GETTING INTO JESUS' LIFE

Beginning Correctly, Finishing Well!

By

John G. Vosnos

TABLE OF CONTENTS

ACKNOWLEDGEMENTS

Warm and deep appreciation to my wife Gayle for her persistent encouragement to write this book and get it published, and to my children, Cynthia, Juliet and Michael for their constant support and for cheering me on. Also, I must extend enormous gratitude to my daughter Juliet for her editing skills and crucial suggestions that enhanced the contents of this book. Finally, special thanks to Dr. Murray J. Harris who long ago urged me to write and publish the things I was teaching and preaching.

INTRODUCTION

Do you ever look at people who call themselves Christians, and wonder about the lack of Christlikeness in them? Have you ever looked into your own life and questioned where you really stood with God? Do you ever entertain the inner suspicion that your relationship with God is pretense, a charade, the mere repeating of the words and feelings of others without internal conviction and change? Perhaps you call yourself a Christian, but don't see any significant difference between yourself and someone who isn't a Christian at all. The Bible is quite clear when it describes a Christian as a person who is a new creation. It says that "old things have passed away and new things have come" (2 Corinthians 5:17). How is it, then, that so many people, who call themselves Christian, see little or no change in their lives? How is it that Christians are so often characterized by conflict and divisiveness, anger and an unforgiving spirit, selfishness and immorality? How can their divorce rate be similar to that of the rest of society? It's bewildering to those both within and outside of the Christian community—how so many people claim to be Christians without a noticeable difference in their lives, and so little impact on their world. Frankly, I find it perplexing that with the large numbers of people who claim to be Christians in the Western world, Christianity's influence seems greatly diminished. Could it be because of a fundamental misunderstanding of the Gospel and what it means to be a follower of Christ? Is there a chance that we have altered the Gospel of Jesus Christ in order to accommodate the preferences of the culture? It seems, these days, that in order to market Christianity to a consumer public, we take measures to make a holy God acceptable to sinful people rather than showing sinful people how to become acceptable to a holy God. In doing so, we have prevented people from entering into a life-changing relationship with Jesus Christ and from becoming fully devoted, Christ-centered followers. Is it possible to embrace a set of beliefs and to hold them as religious preferences, without the relationship to Christ that changes us from the inside out? Have we missed the principal purpose of our salvation, which the Bible describes as life/character transformation, the restoration of the image of God (Christlikeness) within us (Romans 8:29)? I believe so. It seems that we have made the Gospel of Jesus Christ about getting our sins forgiven so that we can get to heaven some day; but in the meantime, have minimized the importance of how we live in this present world. We've left out the most important part—life transformation right now, a relationship with Christ that affects and changes every attitude, every behavior, every relationship we have. I had to have answers to these questions. That is what this book is about.

When I was a young boy, I was told that I needed to accept Jesus into my heart to be my Savior so that I could go to heaven one day. The picture I had was one of getting Jesus into my life to go with me and, in some unspoken way, to serve me, to help me feel better about myself, and to assist me in realizing my dreams. In exchange, I would have to try to please Him with my behavior—church attendance, Bible reading, prayer, and some kind of good deeds or Christian service—and not do anything that would make Him unhappy with me. Consequently, my Christian life became one of duty more than delight, of bartering with God, yet wondering if He really approved of me. In other words, the focus was on me. As time went on, I met many Christians who shared the same perspective and struggled with the same me-centered focus and subsequent doubts. We did not understand that Jesus did not want us to invite Him into our lives, but to deny ourselves and get into His life in a life-transforming way. For me, that was soon to change.

The seed of this book was planted and began to germinate in my mind and heart many years ago when, on sabbatical in Cambridge, England, I was doing study research in *The Gospel According to Mark*. In particular, I was struck by the nature of Jesus' call to discipleship, especially in Mark 8 where He states quite clearly, "If anyone wishes to come after me, let him deny himself, take up his cross daily, and follow me." This invitation, latent with a clear demand, stood in stark contrast to the Gospel of the day in which I lived which attempted to make faith in Christ and following Christ as easy and palatable as possible—a "sugar-coated Gos-pill," so to speak, perhaps in hopes that the ranks of Christianity, and more particularly one's individual church, might swell in number because we had widened the door to everlasting life. The more I considered the nature of Jesus' call to us, the more I realized that His Gospel had been watered down, His grace cheapened by this change.

The idea of *getting into Jesus' life* has given me a perspective that has changed the way I think about being a Christian and how I pursue the Christian life. The thread that ties together the ideas of this book is captured in the title of the second chapter, "Trusting with Abandon." The premise is that Christ does not ask us to invite Him into our lives to help us fulfill our dreams. He does not want us to come to Him for what we can get from Him to enhance our life agenda. Rather, He calls us to deny ourselves and get into His life, following Him (Mark 8: 34, 35). It is in getting into His life that He, in turn, gets into ours and transforms us into His likeness. The self-denial necessary to get into his life requires complete trust, something we do not generate in and of ourselves. *Trust* is a relationship word describing our response to the One who loves us more than we can imagine, One who has gone public in demonstrating the depth of His love for us.

There is a progression to these considerations. We begin with a Gospel different from the self-serving gospel often proclaimed today, a gospel that panders to religious consumerism. The Gospel according to

Jesus is a call to self-denial and a rigorous following of Christ that I have chosen to describe as *getting into Jesus' life.* I can deny myself and follow Christ in this way only if I trust Him with abandon. I can trust Him with abandon if I realize, experience and respond to His overwhelming love for me, a love that accepts me "just as I am without one plea, but that [His] blood was shed for me." Abiding in that love, I abide in Him, in His precious word, the Bible, and love and accept my fellow believers and my neighbors *just as they are.* Christ's likeness is now being formed in me, for God is love. Trusting in His love, I can draw from His life, adopt His servant's heart, embrace His mission and fulfill my calling in the environment of a life that is being transformed by the nature of this relationship with Him. Effectiveness in that mission will be fostered by my participation in Jesus' spiritual regimen or disciplines, in the Scriptures and especially in His persistent praying—disciplines that fueled His spiritual resolve and effectiveness. That regimen will focus my eyes on Christ daily, enabling me to live courageously, respond positively to His mandate to make disciples, run the race with endurance and finish well. When I finish the course, I will see Him face to face, completing the quest I entered by getting into Jesus' life. Then I "shall be like Him for we shall see Him as He is" (1 John 3:2).

For some, this book may prove to be a primer for establishing a relationship with Jesus Christ and beginning the journey of following after Him the way He intended. For those who have been Christians for some time, reading this book may give definition to what Brennan Manning describes as a "second call" that results in a "second journey" in our pilgrimage of faith. He says, "The second journey begins when we know we cannot live the afternoon of life according to the morning program."

With a fresh understanding of the nature of Jesus' call on our lives, Christian faith can no longer be seen as something tacked on to our lives' list of acquisitions, included in the inventory of our lives' accomplishments or added to our portfolios. Rather, it will be an abandonment of confidence in any of these things, and an immersion into the life of the One who loves us immeasurably and who sacrificed His very life to redeem ours. Jesus will no longer be merely a guest in our hearts or a servant of our wishes, but the proprietor of our lives and the possessor of our souls. He will be both Savior and Lord. Then and only then will His joy be in us and our joy be full, just as He promised (John 15:11). The evasive happiness of pleasurable satisfaction that most people chase in a variety of dead-end pursuits will be replaced by the deep-seated joy of a life well-lived in harmony with the creative purposes of God for us. Come with me, then, on a life-changing quest, more than you imagined — getting into Jesus' life.

CHAPTER ONE:

BEGINNING CORRECTLY

The call of Jesus on your life is no small thing. It is not a partial thing. It is everything. The Apostles and earliest followers of Jesus recognized this as they left their relatives and homes, surrendered their jobs, their possessions, their security, and even their lives to follow Christ. The Christian martyrs and reformers who succeeded them were cognizant of the nature of Christ's call. Sister Maria Teresa understood the call of Jesus on her life as she gave herself, in the name of Jesus, to the poor, the downtrodden and dying on the streets of Calcutta. Distaining her own creature comforts, she extended compassionate comfort and aid to the suffering and dying as she cradled them in her arms. Prem Predham knew that the call of Christ was everything. This founder of a home for orphans in India was imprisoned for refusing the government's order to stop sharing the Gospel of Christ. Incarcerated, he became a modern day Apostle Paul witnessing from his tiny prison cell to the guards who were stationed there. As he led them one by one to a personal relationship with Jesus Christ and they told others, new churches were begun. Officials moved him from prison to prison. Each move resulted in new converts and new churches in each city.

Harry Conn, a successful American industrial engineer, also understood this call of Christ. Although he held numerous patents and earned a large income, he chose to live with his wife and children in a small apartment so that from his personal income he could provide total support for sixteen missionaries who were spreading the Gospel of Jesus Christ. These have been joined by the rank and file of Christians throughout the years who have held loosely to this life and their own possessions and personal dreams, in order to answer the call of Christ on their lives.

We might call these people exceptional Christians, perhaps even radical. They would call their actions normal and expected. I think Jesus would too. "[Jesus] interrupts our lives and asks, 'Are you going to spend your life on your own glory, or do you want to live for something greater?' The preeminent temptation of our day is not some nefarious iniquity; it is the subtle, often silent stroll into mediocrity...Into this world, Jesus calls...offering us a life more exciting than anything imagined by the tinseled minds of Hollywood."[1]

For us to respond as we should to the call of Jesus requires us to trust Him with abandon. To trust Christ with abandon, we need to know that He loves us more than we can imagine and has a perfect plan, one that is for our good and not evil, to give us a future and a hope. Those are, in fact, God's very words to us in Jeremiah 29:11. Yet, we are tempted to come to Jesus simply to *get from Him* because we tend to love ourselves so much. We want Him to answer every prayer the way we want it answered; to help us fulfill our dreams; to give us the job we are seeking, or the parking place we need. Even self-deprecating people betray an unhealthy self-love as their disparagements reveal their selfish belief that they deserve to be more gifted or more talented than they are, or to look better than they do. All these are forms of self-absorption. We may even agree to follow Christ and call ourselves Christians in order to get what *we think we need from Him.* When we do that, we are still serving our own interests rather than His and miss what He has planned. We may even find ourselves disappointed with God when things don't go the way we thought they should. At that point, we may question whether God can be trusted in everything—or in anything. These are the issues that Jesus confronts with His first followers. He wanted to make sure they began their relationship, pilgrimage, and adventure with Him correctly. He wants to make certain we do the same.

"And Jesus went out, along with His disciples, to the villages of Caesarea Philippi; and on the way He questioned His disciples, saying to them, 'Who do people say that I am?' And they told Him, saying, 'John the Baptist; and others say Elijah; but still others, one of the prophets.' And He continued by questioning them, 'But who do you say that I am?' Peter answered and said to Him, 'Thou art the Christ.' And Jesus began

to teach them that the Son of Man must suffer many things and be rejected by the elders and the chief priests and the scribes, and be killed, and after three days rise again. And He was stating the matter plainly. And Peter took Him aside and began to rebuke Him. But turning around and seeing His disciples, He rebuked Peter, and said, 'Get behind Me, Satan; for you are not setting your mind on God's interests, but man's'" (Mark 8:27-29, 31-33).

In these verses,

Jesus Confronts a Fundamental Human Problem—SELF.

In Mark 8:15, Jesus had just warned His disciples, "Beware of the leaven of the Pharisees and the leaven of Herod." With these phrases Jesus indicates two life-compromises that were a danger then. The leaven of the Pharisees is empty, superficial, "going through the motions" religion; the leaven of Herod is self-serving ambition, both still very real life-compromises today. Jesus' two-fold warning prefaces one of the most dramatic scenes in Scripture where Jesus spells out what it means for a person to be a true Christian and faithful follower of Christ. Here He shows us that becoming a Christian does not mean inviting Christ into your life. Rather, it means responding positively to His love for you and His invitation to you to get into His life.

The scene opens with Jesus asking a critical question, "Who do people say that I am?" What is the popular opinion of the day about Jesus? The answer the disciples gave is similar to what people today might say. "He is a good teacher, a particular prophet, a good man, a good example." At best, this is a clouded view of Jesus, reducing Him to what uninformed people think of Him. Of course, public opinion doesn't define Jesus. So Jesus presses a more direct and personal question, one you and I must answer ourselves: "Who do *you* say that I am?" What would you say? Peter responds boldly and correctly, "You are the Christ—that is, the Messiah, the One God promised would come to bring salvation to people everywhere—the Son of the living God." What a good confession! This is the starting point for becoming a Christian and getting into Jesus' life. Did Peter and the others understand the implications associated with who Christ is? Do we understand?

Following Peter's good confession, Jesus elaborates what it means for Him to be the Messiah and spells out where His calling is going to take Him. In no uncertain terms, Jesus explains that His is a path of suffering and death. But it included the victory of His powerful resurrection from the dead. You can almost hear Jesus asking, "Is this the life you want to get into? Is this the Christ you want to follow? Is this a path you want to take?"

Immediately we see that Jesus' description of what was ahead did not fit with Peter's plans. Now there is no doubt that Peter was, in some way, following Jesus. He had just confessed Jesus to be the Christ, the Messiah. Yet, even though Peter had left his former vocation and was already following

Christ courageously, apparently he was doing it for the wrong reasons. So were the others (we see that later in their arguments over who would be greatest in Christ's kingdom). You see, just as in a marriage, if you start off on the wrong foot or get married for the wrong reasons, there will be problems down the road. The same is true in our coming to Christ.

Peter reacts to Jesus' talk about suffering and dying. He doesn't even hear the part about resurrection. He grabs Jesus, takes Him aside, and begins to rebuke Him for talking this way. Imagine that! Questioning Christ and the way things are going. We would never do that, would we? What happens next is something we must not miss. As Peter rebukes Jesus, Jesus turns around and sees the other disciples looking on and more than likely, listening in. By turning toward them, He puts His back to Peter— reflected in the literal meaning of the New Testament Greek verb used here, *epistrapheis*, "*turning around, turning one's back on*"—and then rebukes Peter with these stern words: "Get *behind* Me, Satan! You are not setting your mind on God's interests, but on man's"—your own! Peter was now literally where he belonged, *behind* Jesus. Using the term, *Satan,* a term which literally means *adversary* or *one who opposes,* Jesus is describing any activity that demonstrates self-interest and departure from God's will and plans. Such action obstructs God's intentions in a person's life and in the life of His church. Could it be that Peter had linked up with Jesus to serve his own interests? Was he hoping that Jesus would carry out what he, Peter, had in mind for life and the future?

Apparently so. Peter is like so many of us who have notions of how we want life to be. We invite Jesus into our lives to make things better and to bless our plans. We, along with Peter, have a serious lesson to learn if we are to fully understand what it means to be a Christian. Jesus now shows us that following Him involves letting go of self-interests *completely* and requires our getting into His life. In Mark 8:34, Jesus says, "If anyone wishes to come after Me, let him deny himself, and take up his cross, and follow Me." In saying this,

Jesus Calls Us Into His Life, to Follow Him

Understand this: what Jesus is saying to us at the very entry point of becoming a Christian is unquestionably clear. "If anyone desires to be a Christian and determines to identify with Me, come after Me, and have a relationship with Me, he must first *deny himself.*" By this Jesus insists that we let go and lose sight of our own personal interests that prompt us to ask so readily about so many things, "What's in it for me?" As Richard Foster reminds us, "He is calling us to a trust that stoutly refuses to regard self-interest as the highest good in life...In fact, [this] is a frontal attack on all the egocentric hyphenated self-sins of our day: self-indulgence, self-will, self-service, self-aggrandizement, self-gratification, self-righteousness, self-sufficiency, and the like."[2]

Clearly, Jesus confronts the rudimentary problem between people and God, and between people and people for that matter. We want *our* way. The first chapter of the Apostle Paul's letter to the Romans describes it this way: "[We] exchanged the truth of God for a lie, *and chose to* worship and serve the creature rather than the Creator." (Romans 1:25). Jesus' call is a call to repentance, to turn away from one direction in order to go in an entirely different direction. Without this it is impossible to follow Him.

The self that Jesus tells us to deny is not our personhood, but the ego—that prideful part of us that moves us to value our own interests and desires over God's. Peter needed to stop trying to fit Jesus into his life and his plans. He needed to deny himself and his selfish agenda and get into Jesus' life, embracing Christ's agenda. So do we. How? We'll explore that in chapter eight. For now, we must learn and affirm what the Apostle Paul later wrote to Corinthian Christians: "Christ died for all, that they who live should no longer live for themselves, but for Him who died and rose again on their behalf" (2 Cor. 5: 15). This is a declaration that makes it impossible for a person to claim to be following Christ, yet live for himself. It is the difference between building one's entire life on Christ, or simply trying to fit Christ into a self-determined, self-serving agenda. Let me illustrate. In Scripture, Jesus Christ is referred to as the cornerstone. In times past, the cornerstone was the first element to be set in the construction of a building. The trueness of the walls of the building was determined by the cornerstone on which they were constructed. More recently we build buildings based on other technological measures. Today, *after* the building is completed, the cornerstone is set, fitted into the already constructed building as a formality. Similarly, instead of building our lives entirely on Christ and His values and directions, we determine the walls of our lives and then attempt to *fit Christ in* after the fact. Jesus had something very different in mind for us. As Charles Colson explains, "It is an exchange of identities. Christ comes to the cross to die, giving His righteous life for us; we in turn come to the cross to die, surrendering our old sinful life for Him."[3]

So Jesus adds the next essential step for the person who wishes to come after Him. After denying himself, he must "take up his cross." One commentator appropriately translates the word *cross* as *execution stake*. It stands for humiliation and loss — even death. Jesus' call to us to get into His life may well entail all three of these — humiliation, loss, and even death.

Thousands of Christians globally know this first hand today. But we who live in relative ease and affluence may not have a clue regarding this demand — we who sometimes shrink from the embarrassment we may have to endure if we speak up for Christ within our own communities and cultures, on the job, in the classroom, or with our neighbor next door; we who evade the inconvenience of representing the love of Christ to the poor and the downtrodden. We face the temptation to seek worldly security and comfort rather than risk our lives for Christ. By the time Mark wrote this account, the literal cross was a cruel reality both for Jesus and His early followers. Peter himself would later write this: *"Jesus Himself bore our sins in His body on the cross (the execution stake), that we might die to sin and live to righteousness; for by His wounds, you are healed"* (1 Peter 2:24). Jesus' words "take up your cross" are a sober caution that the trust and commitment He is asking from us, foresee no turning back, and call for a willingness, if necessary, to lose everything in pursuit of Christ and His cause. Deny yourself, take up your cross, and, He adds, *follow me*. What is fascinating about these last two words is that they fit so perfectly the scene that is painted here with Peter standing behind Jesus where Jesus had put Him by turning around toward the other disciples. Literally, the phrase means, *"to get in behind and follow the leader."* Remember that childhood game, where the followers did *exactly* what the leader was doing or lost the game? Frankly, Jesus is saying, "My child, get in behind me and follow, walking with me on the same road, going in the same direction, making my agenda yours. Don't try to fit me into *your* life. You get into mine. It is the difficult and narrow way that leads to eternal life."

Now the letters *WWJD, What Would Jesus Do* become both meaningful and demanding. Jesus is speaking of a dimension of *trusting Him* that goes far beyond mere lip-service and rote religious activity and busyness, and becomes a rigorous, relentless pursuit of Christ that let's go of oneself and permeates every nook and cranny of our lives as we embrace Christ's will. It is trust that throws itself on Him in full surrender because He has put His life on the line for us.

I recall sitting spellbound in front of the television as I watched the video of a man perched precariously on an upper story window ledge of a tall building, black smoke and orange flames billowing out of the window behind him, threatening his life. It was only a matter of time before he would succumb to the flames or be forced off the high ledge to his death. Sadly, he was completely out of reach of the firemen's ladders and extensions. Suddenly, from the roof above, a lone fireman was lowered on a rope being held by fellow firemen above. He had to descend through the inferno pouring out of the window in order to reach the desperate man. Finally, as he dangled perilously in front of the man he came to rescue, that man leaped from the ledge and the fireman caught him in his arms. Clinging to the man with adrenaline-fueled strength, the rescuer held him tightly until they were drawn to safety. The drama concluded with a reunion of the firefighter and the rescued victim, who ran to the fireman, embraced him, and affirmed through his tears, "I owe my life to this man. There isn't anything I would not do for him, today, tomorrow—ever!" What a picture of the grateful response we owe to Christ.

If there is, at this point, still any doubt as to what Jesus means, He wraps up this momentous teaching opportunity with these words: "Whoever wishes to save his life shall lose it; and whoever loses his life for My sake and the gospel's shall save it. For what does it profit a man to gain the whole world, and forfeit his soul? For what shall a man give in exchange for his soul? For whoever is ashamed of Me and My words in this adulterous and sinful generation, the Son of Man will also be ashamed of him when

He comes in the glory of His Father with the holy angels" (Mark 8: 35-38). With this declaration,

Jesus Creates the Climate for Our Response

The climate for our response is paradoxical. A person must lose his life in order to save it. The person who attempts to save his life—that is, who clings to his own interests, feathers his own nest and does all he can to make sure he doesn't miss out on things that bring personal gain and self-gratification—that person will lose his life. That is, he will fritter it away and come up empty. Therefore, what shall it profit a man if, in pursuit of his own interests, he gains the entire world, finishes with the most toys, but loses his own soul? On the other hand, the one who is willing to let go of all of that and even lose his life for the sake of a relationship with the Lord Jesus and participation in Christ's agenda—the compassionate care of the downtrodden and the spread of the Gospel—that person will secure life. He will know genuine fulfillment now, and enjoy life everlasting in the glorious presence of Christ Himself.

As I considered all of this, I realized that these statements do not constitute a harsh, unrealistic demand from Christ. Rather, they are a description of love. Can you see that? Christ is asking us to love Him as He has loved us. This is merely a description of what He has done for us in the first place. In the second chapter of the Apostle Paul's letter to the Philippians, we read that Jesus did not cling to His heavenly position, but denied Himself, emptied

Himself, and took up the literal cross of suffering and death for us. In John 10, Jesus calls Himself the Good Shepherd who lays down His very life for the sheep. In Ephesians 5, Christ's love is described as of one who gives Himself up for us, His bride. That is precisely why the Apostle Paul, in Philippians 3:7, 8 also asserts: "But whatever things were gain to me, those things I have counted as loss for the sake of Christ. More than that, I count all things to be loss in view of the surpassing value of knowing Christ Jesus my Lord, for whom I have suffered the loss of all things and count them but cow dung, in order that I may gain Christ." Can we say the same?

We have gone back to the starting point with Jesus. We have seen that Jesus was preparing his first followers and now is teaching us what it means to forsake ourselves and get into His life—to fit our lives, our work, our families, our fun into the framework of His life, His values, His rule, His kingdom. What lies ahead in our pursuit of "Getting into Jesus' Life" holds the prospect of rich benefit to our lives in Christ. But just now, we need to ask ourselves, "Have I begun correctly with Jesus?" How *will* we respond? Jesus loves us more than we know. He wants us to get it right and not be mistaken like Peter and the others were at first. Jesus is saying to us, "I have loved you beyond measure. I forsook all that was mine, everything self-serving, in order to come after you and save you. I was nailed to the cross for you. I laid down my life for you. When I talk about the Son of Man suffering and dying, I am describing the nature of my love for you. If you receive my love for you and come after me, I am simply saying that I want you to love me the same way I love you." The invitation Christ is extending to us here is a far cry from the childish notion of asking Jesus into your heart so that you can avoid hell and go to heaven some day. And He calls to us with a fervency and intensity that is nothing like the pale, namsy-pamsy Jesus pictured in some Sunday school lesson timidly tapping on our heart's door and asking us to let him in. His is a vigorous and robust call to self-denying discipleship—us following Him with unswerving abandon. As the One who can be trusted without a trace of reservation, the Lord is asking you and me to put an end to living somewhere in between. He is calling us to self-forgetfulness, to losing ourselves in the wonder and gratitude of Who He is and what he has done for us. He is urging us to say goodbye to ourselves and hello to everything to which He calls us. He is asking us to assess with simple honesty the reality of our respective situations and then to take whatever steps are necessary to respond to His clear call today. This requires unparalleled trust in Christ—a trust aroused by Christ's enormous love for us. What happens consequently in our lives will not only bring honor and delight to God and deepest satisfaction to our longings, but also will be a clear and radiant picture of Jesus to the people around us who need Him so desperately.

CHAPTER TWO:

TRUSTING WITH ABANDON

P lease let me say it again: responding to Jesus' call and getting into His life calls for unrelenting trust in Him. In fact, the genuine Christian life can be defined not in a sentence, but in a word, *trust;* trust as seen in Proverbs 3: 5,6: *"Trust in the Lord with all your heart, and do not lean on your own understanding. In all your ways acknowledge Him, and He will direct your path."* Have you ever seen a professional wrestler climb to the top of the wrestling ring ropes and then throw himself onto an opponent? That is a picture of this word *trust*. The word for trust in these verses is the body-slam-yourself-on-God variety—a relentless throwing of ourselves on God in total reliance on Him. How else could we possibly respond to His call on our lives to deny ourselves, take up our crosses daily and follow Him? Yet, isn't it true that we do not always fully trust our Lord Christ? Coming to Christ, we are like the seventy-five-year-old fellow whose nephew gave him his first airplane ride for his 75th birthday. When they landed, the nephew said to him, "Well, Uncle Dudley, were you afraid?" "Oh, No-o-o," was his uncle's hesitant reply, "but I never did put my full weight down." We chuckle, but don't our attitudes and actions often say, even without words, "Jesus, I trust you, but only so far"?

Among the reasons for this may well be what Francis Fukuyama has observed in his book titled *Trust,* a fascinating analysis of the role of social trust in the development of cultural prosperity. He writes that the United States has undergone a "rights revolution" in the last half of the twentieth century. This revolution has provided a moral and political basis for the promotion of individualistic behavior, with the consequent weakening of many earlier tendencies toward group life (or community) based on social trust. He goes on to say that this has contributed to the breakdown in relationships, the disintegration of the nuclear family, feelings of social isolation and loneliness, and distrust of others, friend and foe alike. This distrust has been directed toward governmental and other authoritative leadership, and religious tenets, which ultimately translates into a lack of trust in God Himself. The lack of trust in God has resulted in the jettison of God's values, moral code and authority, now seen by many in our society as intolerably repressive and counter to free expression of one's individual rights and entitlements.[4]

In evangelical Christian circles, this shows up in our difficulty to respond to what was once a normal, but is now perceived as a radical call of Jesus to deny oneself, take up one's cross, and follow Him. The climate of our culture and our own natures oppose the idea of laying aside your own rights and prerogatives for the sake of others—especially if doing so entails suffering or loss, or even inconvenience or discomfort. Nevertheless, this is the very path that Jesus took Himself when He entered this world to come to our rescue and redeem our souls. As the Apostle Peter indicates in his first epistle, it is to this that Jesus calls us—to get into His life and follow in His steps. To be able to do this, we must learn and appropriate Jesus' secret—*trusting God with abandon.* In 1 Peter 2:12, after Peter advises us to keep our behavior excellent especially among non-Christians, and urges us in verses 13 through18 to submit ourselves for the Lord's sake to those in authority, whether government or employer or whomever, even if they treat us unjustly, he adds this: "For this finds favor, if for the sake of conscience toward God a man bears up under sorrows when suffering unjustly. For what credit is there if, when you sin and are harshly treated, you endure it with patience? But if when you do what is right and suffer for it you patiently endure it, this finds favor with God. For you have been called for this purpose, since Christ also suffered for you, leaving you an example for you to follow in His steps..." (1 Peter 2:19-21). In so many words, Peter shows us

The Need to Trust God with Abandon

Peter, whom earlier we saw struggling to trust Christ because he wanted his own agenda, Peter, who denied knowing Jesus on the eve of Jesus' crucifixion, really came to grips with the fact that Jesus does not want us to try to fit Him into our lives and plans, but to deny ourselves and get into His life. For Peter, it came together on the shores of Galilee when the risen Christ asked him three times, "Peter, do you love me?" with the underlying implication, "Do you now trust me and my plans and purposes?" When Peter answers, "Yes, Lord, you know I do," Jesus says quite plainly (you can read it for yourself in John 21), "then show it by serving me. Feed my sheep. Serve with compassion. Follow me. And guess what, Peter. That is going to involve your being bound and taken where you don't want to go, and eventually dying for me." Now Peter, who by this time had seen the love of Christ poured out for him on the cross, trusted Christ, denied himself, got into Jesus' life and followed Him, even though it meant suffering and death. He now knew Jesus' secret, and he shares it with us in this passage.

We can summarize Peter's message in this letter this way: "Christians, live godly lives in the middle of cultural confusion and secular opposition, even if that means suffering unjustly, and leave the results, the outcomes entirely up to God. This means you must trust God with abandon like Jesus did." The operative word here is *submit,* first to God, then to others. It is the attitude of a servant. Christ's life is the way of humility and compassion. Yet, isn't a faith that is defined by "asking Jesus into our hearts" in order to have a Savior who meets our needs, at risk of creating a consumer-based relationship rather than one that will transform us into likeness of our servant Savior? Can we see evidences in our lives of self-serving religion? Isn't it true that we often approach the Christian life as consumers, wondering what God will do for us next, or questioning why He hasn't done what we expect? Do we find ourselves choosing churches to attend because of what programs they have to offer; or worse yet, leave because they don't offer what "meets our needs"? Aren't we tempted to keep trying to fit Christ into our lives while at the same time attempting to live so much like the society around us? Yet, Jesus calls us to God-trusting self-denial that is thoroughly counter-culture and will often put us at odds, not only with the culture, but with our own natural tendencies and desires. Nevertheless, it is essential if the character of Christ is going to be shaped within us and the people around us who are without Christ, referred to in verse 12 as pagans, are going to see the reality of Christ's life in us and glorify God.

While Peter is speaking about specific situations where following Christ fully and consistently may result in suffering, he draws an across-the-board application for all of life and ties it directly to the life and example of Jesus Christ Himself and our being called to follow in Christ's steps. Peter had learned this lesson so well that, in so many words, he asserts here in this passage that "the suffering of Christ is a paradigm for Christian existence."[5] Peter knew what we must remember, that Jesus did not live His spiritual life in the safe confines of a church facility, or in the secure surroundings of his private residence. Christ strode boldly into the marketplace and mainstream of his culture and lived compassionately, brightly and unmistakably as the light of God shining into a sin-darkened world. As a result, he drew fire—a lot of it—from both secular and religious sectors, resulting in his being socially rejected, suffering unjustly, and eventually being executed based on drummed up charges. Even as Jesus, betrayed and abandoned by His closest friends, writhed on the cross, His enemies scorned and mocked Him. Peter records Jesus' response to all of this in verses 22: "[Jesus] committed no sin, nor was any deceit found in His mouth; and while being reviled, He did not revile in return; while suffering, He uttered no threats." Jesus did not flinch or waver, fight back or retaliate. He did not assert his rights or complain about what God the Father was doing to Him, nor raise His fist toward heaven for the injustices He suffered. With flint-faced resolve, Jesus pressed forward to do His Father's will. That is the kind of life into which He calls us. But how did He do it? For us to deny ourselves and get into His life and follow, we must learn His secret. Peter reveals it in verse 23: *"He kept entrusting Himself to the One who judges righteously."* Jesus' secret is that He trusted God His Father with abandon. He believed that regardless of how things appeared to be going at the moment, His heavenly Father could be trusted with the outcomes. He knew intuitively what the Apostle Paul later affirms in Romans 8:28, "God causes all things to work together for good to those who love Him and are called according to His purpose." When you and I respond to God with that kind of trust, our lives will be transformed and will shine brightly with the light of Christ's life. Then we will move with selfless compassion into a world broken with selfishness and sin.

In a day rampant with the demand for individual rights, entitlements and personal, if not selfish expectations, together with mountains of litigation in the courts to secure those rights and entitlements, we may find it difficult to understand the course of action Jesus calls us to take in any number of difficult circumstances. Still, He calls us to trust God with such abandon that we will endure hardships, social pressures, and even injustices, not for our own sakes, but for the sake of Christ and His Gospel. As Jesus has taught us clearly, the one who loses his life for Jesus' sake and the Gospel will find it. Trusting God with abandon says, "I will suffer mistreatment without complaint or retaliation, knowing that in doing so, I will display the life of Christ and possibly attract my detractors to Him." This is why Peter can continue this theme in chapter three with a word to wives who have husbands who are disobedient to God's Word and are causing the wives grief. When those wives act on the basis of trust without restraint, their husbands can be won over without a word from their wives as they observe their incredibly Christ-like attitude and behavior. My own mother demonstrated the validity of this. She was a godly Christian woman, but my father was not a Christian. Often, he could be difficult and unreasonable, and seldom supportive of her service to Christ. Yet, uncomplaining, she responded to him with a quiet, gentle, Christ-like spirit, even when wronged. Her confidence rested squarely on the promises of God. She was not disappointed. Her unrelenting trust and consistent spirit were rewarded the day my Dad put His faith in Jesus Christ as his own Savior and Lord.

Trust with abandon, even when suffering unjustly, is why an early church pastor named Polycarp could offer food and drink to those who came to arrest and execute him, and who later burned him at the stake. In A.D. 155, Polycarp was summoned before the proconsul and charged with being a Christian. "Swear," the magistrate urged him in an effort to make him recant his faith and secure his freedom. "Curse and renounce Christ." With unrelenting faith Polycarp replied, "Eighty and six years have I served him, and he has done me no wrong; how then can I blaspheme my king who has saved me?" "I have wild beasts", the proconsul threatened; "If you don't repent I will have you thrown to them." Polycarp responded, "Send for them." In despair at Polycarp's obduracy the magistrate told him, "If you don't despise the wild beasts I will order that you be burned alive." "You threaten the fire", Polycarp told him, "that burns for an hour and in a little while will be quenched; but you are unaware of the fire of the judgment to come, and the fire of eternal punishment which is kept for the ungodly." Polycarp's example of uncompromising trust in the face of death has fanned the flames of faith for persecuted Christians throughout the subsequent centuries.

All of this really fits our entire discussion on trusting God with abandon, because the times you and I find it most difficult to trust God are when life seems unfair—when the heart is torn by an unfaithful spouse; when we receive the news of terminal disease; when the fellow employee who is always "kissing up" to the boss gets preferential treatment; when we lose the job after years of faithful service; when the bottom falls out and there seems to be no where to turn. It is precisely at these times that we need to trust God with abandon, believing in His love for us and in His promises to us. That was the key to Jesus' trust in His heavenly Father. He knew that His Father loved Him beyond description and believed that what His Father had purposed and planned, would come to pass. Jesus was convinced that He did not have to assert His rights, retaliate to unfair treatment, or vindicate Himself. He simply needed to trust in His Father's love, knowing that the Father would vindicate Him, causing everything to work for the good He had purposed. In fact, the writer of the book of Hebrews says of Jesus that although He was God's Son, He learned obedience *through* suffering (Hebrews 5:8). Do we trust God like that? To do so, we need to understand the nature of trusting God with abandon and the truth about the God in whom we are to put that trust.

The Nature of Trusting God with Abandon

Trusting God with abandon begins when we understand how much God loves us, and how much He delights in our trust. Jesus' beloved disciple John writes in his first epistle, "We have come to know and have trusted in the love God has for us" (1 John 4:16). He also writes in that same letter, "Look at the kind of love the Father has for us, that we should be called the children of God. And such we are" (1 John 3:1). It is essential to understand that *trust* is a relational word. It is another word for faith. Unfortunately, *faith* has become a *religious* word that has to do with a system of belief or things we say we believe in — rather academic and sterile. But *trust* is a relational word that has to do with how we respond to a person, in this case, God Himself. *Faith* has become a matter of the head, while *trust* is a matter of the heart. Faith is static. Trust is active. Trust obeys God. In a very real sense, trusting God with abandon is childlike in nature. Let me explain.

When Donna and W.C. Martin of Possum Trot, Texas, adopted from the Texas welfare system two "tough case" children, Mercedes, age four and Tyler, age two, they knew these abused children would find trusting them difficult at best. In a December, 2001 *Reader's Digest* article, "Maybe a Miracle," Skip Hollandsworth recounts the Martin's first supper together with their newly adopted children.

"As the family sat down to a dinner of chicken, potatoes, greens and corn bread, Tyler began stuffing food in his mouth as if it were about to be snatched from him. Mercedes slipped leftovers into a napkin to save in case another meal didn't come."[6]

My own children never saved food from the dinner table for fear that I would not feed them again. They believed in their father's love and promised provision for them. When they were older and were using the family car, even when the gas gauge was broken, if I said the gas tank is full, they did not run to the gas station to make sure. They believed what I told them because they trusted me. Before they had learned to swim, I would call to them from the water to jump into the deep end of the pool, promising to catch and support them. Without hesitation they would take the plunge, believing that I was both willing and able to do so. It was not what they saw, but ME they trusted because they knew I loved them. If they thought for a moment that I did not love them, they would not have trusted me and may have acted like Mercedes and Tyler Martin. Later, Mercedes and Tyler came to know and trust in their adopting parents' love for them and no longer felt that provision for their needs would not be there. They learned to trust with abandon.

Such childlike trust can operate even in the midst of inexplicable pain if we understand the Father's love and purposes. Missionary doctor John White, in his book, *The Fight* illustrates this poignantly as he recalls an incident with his eldest son before his son was even old enough to walk:

"Inevitably, he had his first bad fall, splitting his chin widely with a gash that extended up into the floor of his mouth. We were far from civilization. I had no surgical instruments, only a pair of eyebrow tweezers and household needles and thread. I had no means of relieving pain. Firm hands gripped his tiny form as I inflicted what must have seemed like unbelievable pain on my terrified son. To say my heart was breaking sounds sentimental. Yet his pain was my pain… I agonized over his ordeal as I gripped his tender skin with eyebrow tweezers and jabbed a sewing needle again and again into his chin. But I learned two things. First, that God is not a sadist. He takes no pleasure in our pain. If I, a human father, agonized so deeply over the [necessary] pain I was inflicting on my child, how much more did my Heavenly Father grieve over our sorrows? As Isaiah writes, 'In all their affliction, God was afflicted.' I also discovered that although pain is magnified by fear, it is dramatically alleviated by understanding and trust. I could not convey what I was doing to Scott, but God can and does convey it to us…Trusting [God], I become a collaborator with God in the operations by which He remakes His image in me and deepens my faith."[7]

Trusting God with abandon does not require our having clarity in the situation that brings us suffering. It is resting in the fact that even when present circumstances seem unfair, or calamity has struck, or the future is terribly uncertain, the God who loves you knows the plans He has for you. They are "plans for good and not for evil, to give you a future and a hope." Trust does not demand explanations, but simply turns to and leans on the One who has promised. I like the way Robbie Castleman puts it, "Disciples…learn to trust the Lord they have known in the light when all around is darkness."[8] God says to you, "My precious child, just trust me." And convinced of his love, we do. I was struck by what Dale Vjako, a missionary to France, shared in a church service I attended. After recounting the faithfulness of God to them in their work, he said, "Why do we forget that God is in the business of working things out for good for those who love Him and are called, according to His purpose? He just says, 'Trust me. You don't have to know tomorrow. Just trust me.'"

That makes sense since this is the same God who has already given us every good and perfect gift from above to enjoy (James 1:17) including the very next breath we draw, and has moved heaven and earth to rescue us from the consequences of our sin and selfishness by sacrificing His own lovely Son on the cross to pay the penalty we deserve. Why would we not trust in His love for us? Could it be that we want credit for the good things that come our way while blaming God for the bad? Could it be that we have flawed perceptions of what God is like or have believed faulty caricatures of God from others—a God who is indifferent, capricious, stern or retaliatory? Too often we re-create God in our image, making Him like us. But that re-creation is faulty. Our love is conditional, while His is unconditional. Our love is fickle, while His is faithful. Our fathers, family and friends let us down. God is always there for us. He shows up at our school events; He remembers every anniversary; He doesn't let His work or other interest cause Him to neglect His family. Still, we retain the "fear factor." What will happen if I trust God without reservation?

Will He test my faith by taking my child from me, or by sending me to Africa as a missionary, or by asking me to do any number of things that I don't want to do, things that may move me way out of my comfort zones? And so we determine to stay comfortable by redefining *faith* and *trust* to make them fit the framework of our own thinking. But there is a better way to think and be. We must understand that God's promise to His children to cause *all things* to work together for good calls us to trust Him without reservation regardless of present circumstances.

That is exactly what Jesus did, Peter reminds us. Jesus said to the Father, "Abba, I surrender my will, my ways, my entire life to you without reservation and with unfettered confidence because you are my loving Father." In the Garden of Gethsemane Jesus prayed, "If it is possible, let this cup of suffering pass from me. Nevertheless, not my will but yours be done." And in the midst of excruciating suffering, from the cross he cried, "Abba, dear Father, into your sure hands, I commit my spirit." Getting into His life, we must do the same. And we can, because, as Paul reminds us in Romans 8:15, "We have not received a spirit of slavery...but a spirit of adoption as sons, by which we cry out, 'Abba, Father!'"

There are those who talk about faith as a quantitative thing, as in "if you had enough faith thus and so would happen, you would be healed, your suffering would end," etc. However, trusting God with abandon is not something we generate within ourselves. It is our heart and will response to the Person who loves us more than anybody else does—God who is completely trustworthy and who is both able and willing to do all that he has promised. It is important for us to know the truth about God rather than give in to how we sometimes wrongly imagine Him or how He has been characterized incorrectly by others. That is why Sunday corporate worship and daily personal worship are so critical to this matter of trusting. In worship we review and affirm who God is, what He is really like, what He has promised, what He has done in the past and what He is presently doing. When our picture of Him is clear and true, trust is our only reasonable response. The truth is that God our Father is incomparable in His love, complete in His pardon, thorough in His forgiving and cleansing us, and extremely long on patience. Even in the worst of times, when we turn our backs on Him, He does not, will not, cannot forsake nor abandon us. He is love, and love does not do that. Trust Him. Bank on His love for you. Throw yourself on Him with abandon. But know this: trusting God with abandon does not come by way of Easy Street. In fact, our relative ease and affluence have impeded the progress of our trust that comes by crises of faith or a series of crises of faith. Our trust in God is developed and purified in the crucible of suffering and how we respond when the chips are down. It is in this way that we experience God's faithfulness, grace and mercy in our time of need. Peter, James and Paul all write of this in Scripture. "Welcome testing and trials…count it all joy, because they refine your faith and cultivate Christlikeness in your character." God's ideal for us is that we come to the point of trust where we actually thank God in our troubles because they provide the opportunity to test and refine our faith and display the reality of our relationship to Christ. As the Apostle Paul affirms with confidence, "We who live are constantly being delivered over to death for Jesus' sake, that the life of Jesus also may be manifested in our mortal flesh" (2 Corinthians 4:11). Or, as Eugene Peterson paraphrases this in *The Message,* "Our lives are at constant risk for Jesus' sake, which makes Jesus' life all the more evident in us." In other words, it is not in the easy times but in great difficulty that the reality of our faith in Christ shines most brightly. It is our ability to endure and rejoice in the midst of adversity that reveals "the life of Jesus" to others. It is our response to hardship and suffering that displays the hope we have in Christ that He will provide a better, brighter future. We trust God in all our trials and afflictions because we are convinced that God is at work through our setbacks and difficulties to achieve a future good so great that all present suffering seems like "light and momentary affliction" (2 Corinthians 4:11-17). Again, Peterson so wonderfully paraphrases the thought in *The Message*, "These hard times are small potatoes compared to the coming good times, the lavish celebration prepared for us. There's far more here than meets the eye. The things we see now are here today, gone tomorrow. But the things we can't see now will last forever."

Trusting God with abandon is the issue we encounter each time we are faced with matters of obedience to what God has asked of us in His Word, the Bible, and the subsequent choices and actions that follow. It is a matter of fact that our faith is defined by the choices we make and the actions we take.

Brennan Manning, in his superb book *Ruthless Trust,* reminds us that it is our unrelenting trust that delights the heart of our heavenly Father. Our trusting God with abandon tells Him that we know that He loves us unconditionally and that we trust His love. The thing that gives God more pleasure and joy, honor and glory than anything else is our unfaltering trust in His paternal love no matter what is happening. Our trust with abandon says to God without words, "I believe in you. I believe in the enormity of your love for me and in the integrity of your promises to me. I will not hurt or insult you, my God, my Abba, my precious heavenly Father, by doubting your love for me by not trusting you in everything, in every way." Manning adds, "At first we approach God as ragged desperate beggars would approach the King of kings. Later, discovering how much he loves us, we climb into His lap as children do their Daddy...Our ability to trust Christ is affected negatively by our tendency to measure His unconditional compassion with our fickle, thin, pallid, wavering, conditional compassion. He is not us. He is Jesus, the Christ, the Son of the Living God. Trust Him without reservation for He loves you without restraint!" [9]

Such trust shouts with the Apostle Paul in Romans 8: 31ff. "What shall we say to all of this? If God be for us, who can be against us? He who did not spare His own Son, but delivered Him up for us all, how will He not also with Him freely give us all things? Who shall separate us from the love of

Christ? Shall tribulation, or distress, or persecution, or famine, or nakedness or peril, or sword? In all these things we more than conquer through Him who loves us. I am convinced that neither death, nor life, nor angels, nor principalities, nor things present, nor things to come, nor powers, nor height, nor depth, nor any other created thing shall be able to separate us from the love of God, which is in Christ Jesus our Lord." Can you feel the fervor of these expressions of love, epic in their proportions? In pledging our love to someone, we might speak of crossing oceans, scaling mountains or giving up everything else for that person. But these measures pale in comparison to God's love for us in Christ. God so loved us that He *gave*. He gave us *His very own child, His dear, beloved Son*—that warm little toddler snuggled in his bed, his little leaguer he watched get his first hit, that bright young man over whom he burst with pride at his graduation with honors—God took His own lovely boy and heaped on him all our sins, murders, adulteries, atrocities, our snide or nasty remarks, our petty selfishness and impure thoughts, our ruthless ambitions and self-absorbed indifference and greed, all of this ugliness. The full weight of our sin and guilt hung on Him, crushing his spirit under its awful weight. All the grossness of our sins, both open and secret, all our rejections of God and his love and will for us, were laid on Jesus. And at the height of Jesus' suffering, God the Father had to withdraw His very presence from His dear Son. In holy revulsion to the ugliness of our sins hanging all over the Savior, God the Father turned away, and the fury of His wrath

and judgment against our sins—yours and mine—
was unleashed on Jesus. On that cross, Jesus had to
enter the terrifying darkness of being forsaken by
God. While His physical pain was enormous, the
suffering of His soul, cursed with our sin, was indescribable as he experienced the horrifying ferocity of
God's judgment against our sin which was amassed
on Him. Jesus felt the separation, the blackness, the
deep, immeasurable loss. Imagine the agony of His
Father's heart when, as He sent His Son on a descent
into Hell itself for us, He heard Jesus' excruciating
cry from the cross, the cry of the damned, "My God,
My God, why have you forsaken Me." Why? God
knew all to well why. Because of His love for us—
love that required the infinite Son of God to pay
the infinite penalty for our sins in those agonizing
hours on the cross. In that very hour, nature sympa-
thetically responded as unusual darkness fell across
the land in the middle of the day, and the cold chill
wind of isolation and death swept that lonely hill
where our Savior writhed in anguish of body and
soul, because God so loved, that He gave! Nothing,
nothing at all can separate us from that love which is
in Christ Jesus—unless we, doubting, choose to separate ourselves, preferring *our* agenda, *our* notions
of how life should be, *our* insistence on pursuing *our
own* plans, all leading us away from Christ and His
incomparable love. Yet, when we actually trust God
with abandon, we experience and are overwhelmed
by His encompassing love and compassionate faithfulness. He *does* love us. He *does* come through. And
that generates further trust.

Our Lord's invitations and bidding make absolute sense to us beleaguered pilgrims as we get into Jesus' life and hear His compelling words, "Trust in God and trust in Me. Suffering tests those waters. Trials refine the gold. Deny yourself, take up your cross daily, and follow me. Come unto me, all of you who struggle, labor and are heavily burdened, and I will give you rest and peace for your very souls." May we, you and I, trust Him with abandon.

CHAPTER THREE:

ABIDING IN HIS LOVE

To trust God without restraint is to trust and abide in His love for us. But how does one do that?

For years I had heard about the Grand Canyon, how spectacular it is, how beautiful and breathtaking, how the movement of the sun changes the shadows and colors of the canyon in an artistic display only the Creator Himself could produce. I was told that to see the Grand Canyon was an almost unbelievable experience. But that was the problem. I never had seen or experienced the Grand Canyon. Consequently, all the dramatic descriptions didn't mean much to me. It was a distant thing that I could not really appreciate. Then, one day, I walked to the rim of the canyon and felt my breath stop short as I took in the spectacular view. I spent the rest of the day gazing into the Grand Canyon, moving along its rim to see it from different angles. I watched the sun play with the colors and shadows. It was like nothing I had ever seen before. Now I was experiencing the Grand Canyon for myself.

The love of God is like that. We hear about how wonderful, amazing, uplifting and comforting it is. We read and sing of the wonder of God's love, the scope of God's love, and that no one has or ever will love us like God loves us. But it all seems so factual, so academic, so religious and distant— until that time when we understand and experience God's love ourselves, first hand, and respond to that love deep within our own hearts. I invite you to look with me into the very heart of God. There you will see a familiar face—your own as an object of God's unconditional love. That God loves you and me the way He does, to the extent He does, is truly amazing. In fact, it is life changing. When the truth of God's love sweeps over you, flooding your heart and drenching your mind, emotions and will with its reality, you can never be the same again. It answers the "Why?" question of our existence. It shows us how valuable we are. People who know the love of God personally and intimately know it is a bit of heaven on earth, experiencing the assuring warmth of its rays even during the cold rain of life's realities. They find that they can trust God with abandon and enter into a life-changing relationship with His Son without hesitation. God's love for us becomes the basis of our love for Him and for each other. That is precisely what the Apostle John proposes in 1 John 4: 7-17. He emphatically states two times in this passage that God *is* love, and calls us to abide in God's love by answering three underlying questions. The first question is,

What Is the Nature of God's Love for Us?

"Beloved, let us love one another, for love is from God; and every one who loves is born of God and knows God. The one who does not love does not know God, for God is love" (1 John 4: 7, 8).

The matter is stated plainly: God *is* Love. Here we must be very careful, for many have misunderstood this statement or put an incorrect spin on it. The phrase does not mean love is God. Love does not define God. God defines love. The phrase does not mean that one of God's activities is to love. It is a comprehensive phrase meaning that every action or inaction by God is loving. His love is not romantic infatuation. Nor is it fitful, fluctuating and fickle like so much human love. Neither is it selfish in any way. God's love is His fixed resolve, the determination of His entire being, to seek our best, even at His own expense. That, by the way, is the principle meaning of the New Testament Greek word, *agape—love—*every time the Apostle John uses it in this passage—seeking the good of another, even at one's own expense. Knowing that will help clarify such statements as in verse 7, "Everyone who loves is born of God and knows God." John means everyone who loves like this, with a self-giving, sacrificial love without any selfish agenda of any kind. In this letter, the Apostle John tells us that the very essence of who God is, is holy, sinless, selfless love. Because God *is* love, the love of God is the Christian's guarantee that God will, in fact, cause everything to work together for good—even the consequences of evil or calamity—just as He has promised. From this, the

Christian can conclude that everything that happens to him or her will have a positive outcome in the larger picture. Who else is able to love you like that? This alone should arouse in us trust in God with abandon. As John Stott observes, "This is the most comprehensive affirmation of God's being and nature."[10]

Up to this point, for some of the Apostle John's readers, loving others had been a Christian obligation, a duty, much like it is for many of us. "If you are a Christian and walk in the light, you *must* love one another." But here we are taken to a deeper, more profound motivation. It is the nature and enormity of God's love for us that inspires and motivates our own love for others. If we get into Jesus' life, we can't help ourselves, for He is love. It is kind of a spiritual genetics thing. When we become children of God through trusting in Christ, our heavenly Father's spiritual genetics are poured into us. We begin to look like Him. Peter tells us in 2 Peter 1:4 that we partake of His divine nature. That nature *is* love—and God loves you. Yet, the concept can still seem distant, theological, and academic. We need to let this passage answer a second question.

How Does God Show His Love For Us?

"By this the love of God was manifested in us, that God has sent His only begotten Son into the world so that we might live through Him. In this is love, not that we loved God, but that He loved us and sent His Son to be the propitiation [atoning sacrifice] for our sins" (1 John 4: 9, 10).

God is not "all talk." As we have seen earlier, He *shows* us what his love is like. Verse 9 says, "By this God revealed His love for us by sending His own precious, unique Son into the world so that we could have life." The Apostle Paul says something similar in Romans 5:8. "God demonstrates his love for us in that while we were yet sinners, Christ died for us." Jesus Himself said, "Greater love has no one than this, that a man lay down his life for his friends" (John 15: 13). What is astonishing about God's love for us is that He laid down His life for us when we were not His friends, but rebels. God didn't just say, "I love you." He went public with His love. He gave us irrefutable proof of His love for us by going to the cross for us. The fact that God would die for people who were offending Him with their sins is incredible. No one else loves like that. God's love is the exercise of His goodness toward individual sinners—you and me. He put Himself in the line of fire for our welfare, giving His Son to be our Savior so that we could experience a love relationship with God. Someone has put it so well, "Christ is the unveiling of God's heart."

Reflecting on the nature of God's love, Martyn Lloyd-Jones urges, "Hear the Son crying out in his agony, 'My God, my God, why hast thou forsaken me?' and he literally died of a broken heart. John tells us that when the soldiers pierced his side with a spear, 'Forthwith came there out blood and water' (John 19:34). The heart had burst and the blood had clotted, and there it was—serum and blood clot, because his heart was literally ruptured by the agony of the wrath of God upon him, and by the separation from the face of his Father. That is the love of God. That, my friend, is the love of God to you, a sinner. Not that he looks on passively and says: 'I forgive you though you have done this to my Son.' No, he himself smites the Son. He does to the Son what you and I could never do. He pours out his eternal wrath upon him, and hides his face from him His own dearly beloved, only begotten Son. And he did it in order that we should not receive that punishment and go to hell and spend there an eternity in misery, torment and unhappiness. That is the love of God." [11]

Over and over in the Bible, the Apostle John repeats this theme: "For God so loved the world that He gave His only begotten Son, that whoever believes in Him should not perish, but have eternal life" (John 3: 16). "We know love by this, that He laid down His life for us…" (1 John 3: 16).

In 1 John 4: 10, the Apostle John reminds us that it isn't because we loved God first, because we didn't, but that God first loved us. His love involves remarkable self-giving on His part. God the Son identified with our situation to such an extent that He took on himself the sin that sentenced us to eternal death, and He died in our place. That is what John means when he says that God sent His Son to be the *propitiation* [atoning sacrifice] for our sins. It means that on the cross, Jesus Christ absorbed the awful wrath of God's judgment against our sin. During His life on earth, by his perfect obedience to God the Father, Jesus Christ satisfied all the moral requirements of God for holiness and purity. He offers to you and me the credit for His perfection, while suffering, dying and paying the debt for our sin. While we were not loving God, He loved us anyway and took drastic measures to remove the offense that prevents us from having a relationship with Him. As a result, we can be pardoned and forgiven, and we can get into His life. By dying for you, He shows you tangibly how much he loves you and how infinitely precious you are to Him. As you turn to Him and open your heart to receive what He has done for you, He will let you experience the kind of love He has for you. That is the goal of His love for us, to restore us to a warm, personal, fully forgiven relationship with Him and to arouse in us an unrelenting trust that moves us to let go of ourselves—because it is ourselves, our prideful egos, that weigh us down—and get into Jesus' life. In that relationship, we are recreated into the image of God, which is the likeness of His Son, Jesus. When God forgives, He forgets. That is, He no longer relates to us on the basis of our obstructing sin. He wraps His love around us forever. His love wants us to enjoy all that He has for us perpetually. As an old hymn says so well, *"Loved with everlasting love, led by grace, that love to know. In a love which cannot cease, I am His and He is mine."* That brings us to the third underlying question answered in this passage.

What Does the Love of God for Us Mean to Us?

"No one has seen God at any time; if we love one another, God abides in us, and His love is perfected in us. By this we know that we abide in Him and He

in us, because He has given us of His Spirit. And we have seen and bear witness that the Father has sent the Son to be the Savior of the world. Whoever confesses that Jesus is the Son of God, God abides in him and he in God. And we have come to know and have trusted in the love which God has for us. God is love, and the one who abides in love abides in God, and God abides in him. By this, love is perfected with us, that we may have confidence in the day of judgment..." (1 John 4: 12-17).

Father Jim was known as a most godly, loving and caring man. All the children in the orphanage he directed loved him instantly. After they grew up and left the orphanage they would return to visit him and experience his warm love. His uniqueness rested in his ability to accept and even glorify in each child the very thing the child hated most about himself or wished could be different, whether it was unruly hair or big feet or crooked teeth, or whatever. One day, when Father Jim was in town shopping, a new boy arrived at the orphanage. He had severe burn scars that covered half his face. The ridicule and rejection he had received over it had shaped his ornery and defensive disposition, displayed in his unmanageable behavior with the social workers who brought him to the orphanage. As the new boy stood off by himself, defiant of everyone, the other children wondered what Father Jim would do when he returned. Surely he would not be able to find anything good about this boy. They all grew silent when Father Jim pulled up in his car. They stood aside as he got out and noticed the new boy. "Well, who's this?" Father Jim exclaimed as he smiled warmly. "It's a new boy," came a reply. "Well, well, well," Father Jim mused as he approached the defiant lad. Then he caught sight of the awful disfiguration. "Here we go," Father Jim said merrily. And he scooped the boy up in his big arms and kissed him right in the middle of the scarred cheek. Then he hugged him tightly before setting him down. It wasn't long before that boy's disposition changed entirely, because Father Jim's acceptance and love convinced him that even his scars were something special given to him by God. After all, Father Jim had kissed them, and that made them beautiful. Such is the love of God.

God's love for us means we can go further than just knowing about God's love.

We can experience it and abide, or live in it, and actually love each other in the same self-giving way God loves us.

To actually abide in God's love, it is extremely important for you to know that Jesus loves you—I mean, really loves you—thoroughly and completely, no matter what you have or have not done. While others may reject you or set up false standards for your behavior, or accept you conditionally, Jesus accepts you just as you are. He embraces you and kisses you right on your "scars." As someone has said so well, on the cross, "Jesus paid a debt He did not owe, because you owed a debt you could not pay." Jesus loves you right now, this very minute. He extends to you His compassionate spirit, His mercy and His love just as you are. You do not need to change, stop sinning, become religious or do anything to *get* Him to love you. When a wealthy young man rejected Jesus and walked away from Him because he preferred his property to Jesus, did Jesus' love for Him diminish? No. The Bible says that "Jesus felt love for him" (Mark 10: 21). That is unconditional love. Jesus loved the diminutive Zaccheus while he was still a thieving tax collector. The pious and the self-righteous judged Zaccheus, resented him, rejected him and isolated him from themselves. But Jesus, full of compassion and mercy, said to Zaccheus, "I want to come over and have supper at your house today" (Luke 19: 5). Jesus loved Zaccheus just as he was. But he loved him too much to leave him that way. Zaccheus trusted in Christ and accepted Christ's acceptance of him. When Zaccheus, by faith embraced Christ's love for him, he let go of his devious way of life. His direction, business dealings, behavior and everything else totally changed.

How often our academic, cerebral understanding of God's love leaves us out on a limb like Zaccheus, curious about Jesus, but interested from a distance, tenuously clutching our tree branch, unable to let go of our fears, our own pursuits, our self-absorption that place us in such a strange and precarious place. And when Jesus comes along, does he say, "Hang on and make room, I'd like to join you up there"? No, he says, "Let go, come down out of that tree. I love and accept you and want to show you how much. But you have to come down and follow me." Only from Jesus is there love and acceptance to the max. And He loves you. He showed it by laying down His life for you. He beckons, "Come unto me, not to the church, not to a group, but to me. Come angry, come anxious, come wounded and broken, and I will love you and alter you forever. Come in your brokenness, your need, your pain." Do you realize whom it is who is calling you to deny yourself and follow Him? It is not a friend, a parent, or a spouse. It is the Son of God who has come to you with deepest compassion. He is torn with your pain and need. He longs to touch you, show you His love and His life and invite you into it. When we accept His acceptance of us, we are then free to merge into His life and experience his pardon, forgiveness, compassion, direction and intimacy. In other words, we experience a deep down relationship with Him. By getting into His life and His love, He gets into ours.

Getting into Jesus' life and abiding in His love is letting Jesus come to you on *His* terms, full of compassion and love, letting Him embrace you and take you with Him on the incredible journey of the Christian life. We tend to impersonalize His love by saying, "Sure God loves me. He loves the world of which I am $1/6,000,000,000^{th}$ of a part." Do we forget that the God who loves the world is the God who is able to focus so intensely on the individual person that he knows the number of hairs on your head? He who called out the countless stars of the universe by name, sees the little sparrow on one small planet in that universe fall to the ground, and then says to you, "Are you not worth much more to me than a sparrow?" (Matthew 10:29-31) Do we understand such love? His love for you is intensely individual and personal. He loves *you*. He died for *you*. If you were the only person who had ever strayed and sinned against God, He still would have come to rescue you, to die for you, because He loves you—YOU! The Bible says that there is a celebration party in heaven for each individual who turns from his sin, trusts in Christ and gets into His life to follow him (Luke 15:10). Are you a Christian? The day you trusted in Christ, there was cheering and high-fives all around in heaven over you.

It is often said that the worth of an object is determined by what someone is willing to pay for it. Let me ask you, "What price did Christ pay for you?" He paid His own dear life—His precious life-blood (1 Peter 1:18, 19). God loves you that much. This is someone you can trust, someone you want to trust. He is someone you can throw yourself on with abandon. Abide in His love.

The love of God is personal, warm, and healing to us. For example, here is a young person whose father has just walked out and whose mother in her bitterness is drinking too much. Although only fourteen years old, the girl is on her own. But through the faithfulness of certain Christians, this girl discovers God's love for her and hears Him say, "I will be a father to the fatherless. Let me be your Dad and Mom. I love you unconditionally." In a prayer of faith, she trusts in God's love for her shown to her on the cross. Turning from her sin, she tells Christ she will follow Him, and Christ fills her life with His Spirit and His love. Now,

God is not her adversary in bad times. He is her friend and her cure. In the face of feeling abandoned and alone, she hears Christ say, "I will never leave you nor forsake you." Christ wins her love by filling her with His. He tells her that He knows what it feels like to be alone and rejected, but that He will love her and stay with her. He reassures her that even if she walks through the valley of the shadow of death, she does not need to be afraid. He will be with her all the way. She can count on it because He has already proven His love by dying for her. She reads the Bible and it tells her that nothing can separate her from God's love for her. She learns that she cannot screw up so badly that God will stop loving her or adjust His love for her downward. Nothing she says, nothing she does, nothing within her or outside of her can stop the loving. Her heart is filled with God's unconditional love. Do you know what happens next? She begins to share that love with others around her. She just can't help it. Of course she can't, because

God's love in us means that we will love other people with His love

That is where this passage, 1 John 4: 7-17, began: "Beloved, let us love one another, for love is from God...." When we accept God's love for us and accept His acceptance of us in Christ, He puts His love within us so that we can live in it and it can become a part of who we are. So much so, that Jesus tells us that love is the distinguishing mark of the person who has really gotten into His life. 1John 4: 12 tells us that although no one sees God physically, when we love others, God's love becomes visible and real to them as they see it in us and feel it from us. That is why it is so important that Christians engage in unsolicited acts of love and kindness within their spheres of influence. We can go out among the people of our communities to *show* God's love in practical, self-giving ways. They will respond and will be more prone to listen to the Good News we have to share about pardon from sin and new life in Christ. God's love in us uses our hands, arms, words, actions and expressions to get through to others. But there is a key. We abide in Him and in His love. Then His love abides in us. We get into His life, and He gets into ours—and it shows.

At this juncture it is important that we not hear all of this as merely a theological description of God's love or a hollow demand for Christians to love each other. Rather, we must see this as an affirmation of what inspires such love in the first place. 1 John 4: 19 says clearly, *"We love because He first loved us."* The reason we love with God-style love is because He loved us first. It is God's love, not laws or religious regulations that inspires reflex Christian love in us. Genuine, willing Christian living is triggered only in response to the abundant love of God. For too many of us, our Christian outlook and behavior is shaped by the possibility of God's disapproval or anger, not by the enormity of His love and grace. For such people, being a Christian means finding out what the minimum requirements are and then trying to follow those regulations. This attitude is aided and abetted by legalistic Christians who impose non-biblical standards on themselves and others, or by Christian leaders who use fear and guilt to manipulate others. But the Apostle John gives us a better way, God's way. In verse 16 he writes, "We have come to know and have trusted in the love God has for us. God is love, and the one who abides in love abides in God, and God abides in Him." We don't earn God's love, favor and acceptance. Neither do we retain them by the things we do. In Christ we have these already. We abide in love and stand in grace. Our awareness of God's enormous love for us engenders our trust with abandon. When we trust Him with abandon, we enter freely into His life and participate fully in His agenda for our lives. When we do, we love others. "By this," John adds in verse 17, "love is perfected or completed with us that we may have confidence in the Day of Judgment." It is that simple—and that profound.

CHAPTER FOUR:

DRAWING FROM HIS LIFE

By abiding in Christ's love, I can draw from his life. How often have you thought or said out loud, "If only I could *see* God and *hear* His audible voice. If only Christ were still among us and I could walk with Him and talk to Him face to face—then I would be a better, more productive Christian; then, the likeness of Christ would be more clearly developed in me"?

On the night before His awful death, Jesus knew that He had only a short time left with His followers. When His physical presence was gone, what would they do? In the upper room, where Jesus shared with them the last supper and gave them what we call communion, He also gave them His final instructions in what is often referred to as His *farewell discourse* recorded in The Gospel of John, chapters thirteen through sixteen. Here He washes the disciples' feet and then commands them to love and serve one another as He has loved and served them. He describes the difficulties, trials and tribulations that would come to any who follow Him. But He also promises them the gift of the Holy Spirit who would lead them into all truth and remind them of all Jesus had taught them. He knew that getting into His life and living the life to which He had called them, and to which He now calls us, would not be easy. How would they do when He was gone? How would we do? Jesus knew how easy it would be for us to neglect our relationship with Him without His physical presence. He also knew how prone we would be to go it on our own or drop out altogether. There was one matter He needed to explain plainly, a secret for living this life that they needed to understand.

Jesus had a vision for those who followed him, a passion, a dream. As they left that upper room, and walked toward the Garden of Gethsemane, Jesus took them past a vineyard en route to the Mount of Olives. Pointing to the vines and branches and grapes, Jesus prepared His first disciples, and now us, for living the Christian life without His physical presence, by sharing with them the secret for success in three words. Not, *bear much fruit,* as we industrious American Christians are prone to mistakenly emphasize, but these three: *Abide in Christ.* In this timely teaching moment, using this natural vineyard illustration, Jesus explains what *abiding in Christ* is, and why it is essential that we abide in Christ in order to get into His life and have His life get into us. First, Jesus indicates that

Abiding in Christ is a
Life-giving Relationship

Jesus says, *"I am the true vine, and My Father is the vinedresser. Every branch in Me that does not bear fruit, He takes away; and every branch that bears fruit, He prunes it, that it may bear more fruit. You are already clean because of the word which I have spoken to you. Abide in Me and I in you. As the branch cannot bear fruit of itself, unless it abides in the vine, so neither can you, unless you abide in Me. I am the vine, you are the branches; he who abides in Me, and I in him, he bears much fruit; for apart from Me you can do nothing. If anyone does not abide in Me, he is thrown away as a branch, and dries up; and they gather them, and cast them into the fire, and they are burned* (John 15:1-6).

Jesus begins, *"I am* the *true* vine." This is the last of seven *"I am"* statements by which Jesus describes Himself and reveals the nature of His life and ministry—

I am the Light, *I am* the bread of Life, *I am* the Door, *I am* the Good Shepherd,

I am the Resurrection and the Life, and before Abraham was, *I am.*

Here He says,*" I am the True Vine."* People may attach themselves to all kinds of things or people in search of meaning, satisfaction and significance in life. Only Jesus is the *true vine.* He continues, "You are the branches." While the analogy of the vine and branches suggests the importance of fruit-fulness in the Christian life, clearly what Jesus is

emphasizing here is the significance of a relationship—a life-giving relationship with Christ Himself.
Immediately, we sense that in this relationship, the
branches, Christians, are dependent upon the vine,
Christ, for life and nourishment. In fact, Jesus has
said as much already with the words *"As a branch
cannot bear fruit of itself, unless it abides in the vine,
so neither can you, unless you abide in Me."* As we
will see shortly, the nature of one's relationship with
Jesus determines the quality and productivity of the
life. Be sure to notice in verse 1 that Jesus includes
in this analogy a wonderful dimension we often miss
or misunderstand: *"My father is the vinedresser"* (or
caretaker). The caretaker of the vineyard tends to the
vineyard by taking action to maximize the possibility
of a healthy relationship between the branches and
the vine that results in the life of the vine flowing
freely into the branches to secure fruitfulness. Since
Jesus is the Vine and we Christians are the branches,
imagine the implications. Imagine the very life of
Jesus Himself, His character, His wisdom, His truth,
His morality, His integrity, His passion, His compassion, and His purity, flowing in your veins and
filling your mind and soul. Later, the Apostle Peter,
grasping these implications, would write in 2 Peter
1:3, 4, "God has granted to us everything pertaining
to life and godliness...in order that by them you
might become partakers of the divine nature." This
incredible possibility is what God the Father, who is
the caretaker of the vineyard, desires for each of us.

At this point it would be good for us to remember
that our Heavenly Father is deeply invested in

Christians. In light of the biblical statement *"Where a man's treasure is, there will his heart be also,"* think of where God's heart is. He invested the very lifeblood of His precious Son to bring us into this life-giving relationship with His Son. With such a treasure invested in us, we Christians are where God's heart is. Therefore, in the words of the Apostle Paul, *"If God did not spare His own Son, but gave Him up for us all, will He not also with Him freely give us all things?"* (Romans 8:32)

A member of the church where I was a pastor some years ago, whose family owned vineyards in California and Europe, shared with me information about caring for vineyards and grape production. What he said revealed fascinating insights into this analogy that Jesus used to instruct us about getting into His life so that His life can get into ours abundantly. In each of the three relationships described in John 15:1-6, the Father as caretaker of the vineyard takes appropriate actions, actions by which we can be greatly encouraged. In reality, this entire section is about God's gracious tending of this vineyard and His nurturing of the relationship between Jesus the Vine and believers, the branches. In your mind's eye, come with me to a vineyard to see what the Father does in each of these relationships.

The first relationship is described as, *"Every branch in me that does not bear fruit..."* Notice that this branch is *in the vine* but is unproductive. I learned that in a vineyard, this is typically true of branches that, because of winter harshness or some other effect, are drooping downward off the vineyard trellis and lying on the ground. As a result, they begin to send out little tendrils to attach themselves to earth, attempting to draw sustenance directly from the earth and no longer from the vine. Such activity compromises the branch's relationship to the vine and the vitality that comes from the vine. Branches in this situation either bear no fruit at all, or at best, hard, bitter berries instead of full clusters of grapes. What does a vineyard caretaker do with such branches? Jesus says it clearly. *"He takes away."* Even though some versions of the New Testament translate this word, *"to cut off,"* the meaning of the New Testament Greek verb *airoh* means literally, *"to take away or lift up from the ground."* Let me illustrate.

A colleague pastor I know was on a tour bus in Israel somewhere near Hebron when he suddenly jumped from his seat and shouted, "Ralph, stop the bus. Look, John 15:2!" He directed the attention of the other passengers to a nearby vineyard where caretakers were bending down to gently lift tender branches that were lying on the ground, placing them on the trellises and securing them there. In the process, the caretakers were breaking the branches' attachments to the earth, attachments that compromised their relationship to the vine. By lifting them up, they were restoring them to a place in the sun where they would once again draw life from the vine and become productive.

This is exactly what God our Heavenly Father as the Caretaker of the vineyard does with believers who have become attached to the earth and are no longer depending on the Lord Jesus for the life to which He has called us. He does not cut them off. Rather, with grace and mercy, He tenderly reaches down and lifts them up, restoring them to that warm place in the sunlight of His love for them. In doing so, He begins to break their attachments to the things that compromise their relationship to the vine and rob them of spiritual health and productivity. Sometimes this process is painful, but it is always necessary. How often we complain about difficulties, setbacks and losses. Yet, frequently, they are the result of God our Father's loving desire to break our attachments to certain things or people that compromise our relationship with Christ. It is part of His gracious lifting to restore us to the place where we can be enjoyably productive.

In researching this process further, I visited Internet sites on vineyards, grape-growing and the production of wine. There I found pages of instructions on lifting branches from the ground, a process that is also referred to as *training* the branches to grow upward. The branches are lifted away from attachments to the earth, and trained to grow upward toward the sun and inward deeply into the vine. It is then that they begin to bear the desired fruit. That is the next matter to which the Father as caretaker tends—fruitfulness, or productivity.

Every branch that bears fruit, He prunes it to become even more productive. The Greek word here translated *prunes,* is the word from which we get our word *catharsis*. Literally, the word means "cleanses" or "purges" which, of course, is the function of pruning. I learned that branches from the grapevine have a tendency to keep generating new tendrils that go in all directions at once. Such activity robs the original branch of energy and resources needed to produce rich clusters of grapes. If these extraneous growths are not pruned off, they compromise the productivity and abundance of the branch that is bearing fruit. This is precisely what our Heavenly Father does for us when things extraneous to the Christian life compromise our fruitfulness. In John 15:3, Jesus indicates how this pruning or cleansing takes place by saying to His disciples, "You are already clean (or pruned) by the word I have spoken to you." The Scriptures are useful in pruning. That is why for people who are getting into Jesus' life and following Him, reading and thoughtful study of the Bible will actually have the effect of cleansing out things in the life of a Christian which are not in harmony with God's will for us. Elsewhere Jesus says, *the truth will set you free*. Paul calls it *the washing of water with the word* (Ephesians 5:26). The Psalmist writes, "How shall a person keep His way clean? By keeping it according to God's Word. Your Word I have engrafted into my heart, that I might not sin against You." God's word actually has a pruning effect on the true believer. That is why we need to be diligent to take it in, believe it, apply it and do it. This will clear out the extraneous things in our lives which would disease us, sap us of spiritual strength, or detract from our productivity. You see,

Abiding in Christ is a life-giving relation-ship lovingly cared for by our Heavenly Father, the Caretaker of the vineyard. The bottom line to all of this is that God the Father is not sitting back with

His arms folded waiting for us to try our hardest to measure up to His unreasonable expectations. He is proactive in our relationship with Christ. He lifts up, breaks attachments, retrains us, and prunes off the unnecessary so that we can benefit fully from our relationship to the vine and be completely dependent on Christ. The Apostle Paul understood this process, even when it was deeply painful. As he writes about the serious affliction he suffered that almost cost him his life, he says in 2 Corinthians 1:9, *"We had the sentence of death within ourselves in order that we should not trust in ourselves but in God who raises the dead...."* He was able to see how even life-threatening afflictions and disappointing setbacks can be part of God's loving action toward us to foster a relentless trust in Christ that leads to the abundant life. However, in John 15:6, Jesus mentions one more possibility.

The one who does not abide in Christ

"If anyone does not abide in Me, he is thrown away as a branch, and dries up; and they gather them, and cast them into the fire, and they are burned."

The church member I mentioned earlier, whose family owned vineyards, told me of another measure taken in vineyards that relates directly to this condition of one who does not abide in the vine. He described to me the practice of the caretaker who notices a branch that is dry and withering on the vine. The caretaker takes his penknife and probes the juncture where the withering branch intersected the vine. If there is resistance to the probe of the knife, the caretaker concludes that the branch is, in fact, growing into the vine and is probably in need of lifting up or pruning. However, more often the blade of the knife will move easily right through the juncture of that branch and the vine, indicating that the branch is not joined to the vine. It has not gotten into the life of the vine. It is, at best, superficially attached instead of being deeply entrenched. Consequently, the life of the vine has not gotten into the branch. Tossed aside, it dries up completely, and later is gathered up and burned. Do we need to elaborate? In all His tenderness and love, the Master could not avoid solemn words of warning. The person who is not connected with Christ or is only superficially attached is in imminent danger. It is not the branches that *are* in Christ but are not bearing fruit that are cut off and burned. It is the ones that are not attached at all. On the other hand,

Abiding in Christ Produces Christian Character and Productivity

In John 15:5, 7, Jesus says, *"I am the vine, you are the branches; he who abides in Me, and I in him, he bears much fruit; for apart from Me you can do nothing...If you abide in Me, and My words abide in you, ask whatever you wish, and it shall be done for you."*

Notice how fruitfulness and answered prayer are equated with this relationship of abiding in Christ.

Fruit is the outward expression of the inward nature. It is difficult to identify a barren branch, but the fruit on the branch tells the story. In fact, in the broader context of John 14-16, Jesus speaks of His Holy Spirit actually coming and being in us, producing the life and ministries of Christ in us. This certainly does not sound a lot like teeth-gritting self-effort, does it? The Apostle Paul actually describes the fruit that Christ's life in us produces, the productivity that comes from abiding in Christ and having Him and His Word abiding in us by His Spirit: *Love, joy, peace, patience, kindness, goodness, faithfulness, gentleness, self-control* (Galatians 5: 22, 23). You see, when we get into Jesus' life and abide in Him, the inward nature or life flowing into us is Jesus, and the outward expression of that nature, that life, is this fruit. Please notice that the branch does not **produce** the fruit, it bears the fruit produced from abiding in the vine, which is Christ. In fact, Jesus is very clear when He says, "Apart from Me you can do nothing." Of course, He is not referring to our ability to go to work, drive a car, eat a meal, or whatever. He is simply stating that we cannot produce the fruit of Christ's character and ministry within ourselves by our own efforts. "Hey, American, pull-yourself-up-by-your own-bootstraps, Yankee ingenuity, I can do it myself Christian—you cannot do it alone!" Apart from this deeply entrenched, ongoing relationship with Christ, you cannot produce the abundant life that comes only from Christ. Let the Father have His way. Stay connected to the vine, and this relationship will produce Christian character and productivity.

God will be honored by your life in Christ and you will be deeply satisfied because,

Abiding in Christ Brings Glory to God and Joy to the Christian

"By this is My Father glorified, that you bear much fruit, and so prove to be My disciples. Just as the Father has loved Me, I have also loved you; abide in My love. If you keep My commandments, you will abide in my love; just as I have kept My Father's commandments, and abide in His love. These things have I spoken to you, that My joy may be in you, and that your joy may be made full" (John 15: 8-11).

It goes without saying that when we bear the fruit of Christ's life in us, God is honored, magnified and glorified in our lives—fulfilling the principle purpose of our salvation. Jesus says repeatedly that people will know we are His disciples by our uncommon love, our uncanny unity and by our deeds of goodness. People see the reality of Christ in us, are struck by the difference, and are pointed to God. Where does our joy come in this? When I read verse 9, I am absolutely amazed and joy wells up within me. *"Just as the Father has loved Me, I have also loved you; abide in My love."* How much do you think the Father loves the Son? He loves Him immeasurably. Now look at what Jesus says about His love for us—for you. "As the Father has loved me, so I have loved you." Can you imagine that? This is most remarkable that Jesus compares His love for us to the Father's love for Him. Wouldn't you agree that to be loved like that brings joy?

At this point you might be tempted to ask that while this vine and branches and caretaker picture is a wonderful analogy and beautiful portrait of our relationship with Christ, how does a person actually do this? If God's desire is for us to abide in Christ, how can I be sure I am responding correctly? Those are good questions.

To abide means literally *to remain, or to continue on.* Abiding in Christ is a personal, developing, deeply rooted relationship with Christ that is tended and grows and matures. When a person becomes a Christian by trusting in the death and resurrection of Jesus Christ for pardon from sin, when that person decides to follow Christ and get into His life, this marks the beginning of a life-giving relationship. To abide in Christ means to continue on and progress in that relationship, intentionally cultivating the relationship from our side of it. How? We do that very much like any people do who love each other and actively pursue a love relationship with each other. We desire to know more about that person. And if we cannot be together face to face, we correspond in other ways. If the one we love writes to us, we eagerly read what he or she has written, going out of our way to do so, poring over every word and eagerly responding in love however we can. If they send us a card, or a story, or an article, we treasure it because by these they are communicating something they want us to know. If we can telephone them too, that is all the better. I recall how substantial my telephone bill was when, after a move to a new ministry, my wife and I had to live apart for six months! So it is with Christ and us. He has given us His written word, the Bible, which tells us what He is like, how much He loves us, and which unfolds the desires of His heart for us. Jesus says to us, '"*Abide in my love,*" which is another way of saying *"Abide in me."* He also tells us how to do this, "If you keep my commandments, you will abide in my love, just as I have kept the Father's commandments and abide in His love." Because we love Him, trust Him with abandon, and depend completely on Him, we respond positively to what He has to say and what He asks us to do. We pick up the telephone of prayer and talk directly to Him every day, consulting Him about every choice, every attitude, and every action. The implication is a life lived in constant close communion with Christ, day by day, hour by hour, moment by moment, as we proactively cultivate our relationship with Him. Such abiding in Christ involves a tireless pursuit of association with Christ, at times perhaps resembling the Spirit of Jacob who wrestled with the Lord relentlessly, making this appeal, "I won't let you go until you bless me!" (Genesis 32:26.) More specifically, it will involve our diligence and devotion in tending to the pursuits which contribute to our abiding in Christ — prayer, Bible-reading, meditation and reflection, corporate worship with God's people, and celebrating with them Christ's sacrifice by means of Communion, the Lord's Supper. (We will explore these ideas more completely in chapter ten when we discuss our engaging in Jesus' spiritual regimen.)

It is then that we discover the reality of His Holy Spirit within us who speaks into our hearts and applies God's truth. We learn that this is the way the Lord abides in us. We trust and obey and find the Lord faithful and true. The relationship grows and we become more and more like our Lord Himself as His life is reproduced in us. A portrait of Christ develops within us. Then the fruit of His character and service is produced, God is glorified in our lives and our joy is almost more than we can contain. Should we get distracted or tempted away, our Heavenly Father tugs, lifts, and prunes us to get us on track again. Because we love Christ and desire that relationship with Him, we cooperate and respond positively to God's loving, restorative work in our lives. Then God's dream for us becomes a reality—we are indeed a people who abide in Christ and draw our very lives from Him. Ironically, drawing life from Him involves entering into His death and resurrection, as we shall see next.

CHAPTER FIVE:

ENTERING INTO HIS DEATH AND RESURRECTION

Undoubtedly, the imagery of the vine and the branches underlies a favorite expression the Apostle Paul uses repeatedly to describe the nature of a Christian's relationship to the Savior, the potent prepositional phrase, *in Christ*. As John Stott explains, "To be 'in' Christ does not mean to be located inside him or to be locked up in him for safety, but rather to be united to him in a very close personal relationship...to enjoy a living and growing relationship with him."[12] This brief expression, *in Christ,* which occurs over and over in all of Paul's writings, confirms the concept we have been developing, that becoming a Christian involves getting into Jesus' life—abiding in Him. Now we will see that getting into Jesus' life, or being *in Christ*, involves a mystical spiritual union with Christ that includes vicariously entering into

Christ's death and miraculous resurrection from the dead to our eternal benefit, freedom from sin, newness of life now, and the hope of our own resurrection from the dead to life everlasting.

When God the Father sent Jesus into the world, He sent Him for the cross. Throughout Jesus' time on earth, the cross always loomed ahead. His life of perfect obedience to His Father's will led Him inexorably to Calvary. As the day of His destined encounter with crucifixion drew near, Jesus, understanding the necessity of the cross, "set His face like flint" (Isaiah 50:7) in unflinching resolve to experience the horror of that cross and God's wrath directed against our sin and guilt, which He took upon Himself.

The Apostle Paul understood, experienced for himself, and presses upon us the importance—the centrality—of the cross of Christ to our living the Christian life. Here is how he puts it. "Far be it from me that I should boast except in the cross of our Lord Jesus Christ by which the world has been crucified to me and I to the world" (Galatians 6:14 ESV). Again, Eugene Peterson's paraphrase of this verse in *The Message* helps us understand its meaning: "For my part, I am going to boast about nothing but the cross of our Master, Jesus Christ. Because of that cross, I have been crucified in relation to the world, set free from the stifling atmosphere of pleasing others and fitting into the little patterns that they dictate." For Paul, the cross of Christ represented the end of an old way of living life in this world—the society of unbelievers—and the beginning of a whole new way of living that separated him from this world's temporal values and self-centered ways.

However, as Thomas a' Kempis observed many years ago, "Jesus has always many who love His heavenly kingdom, but few who bear His cross. He has many who desire consolation, but few who care for trial. He finds many to share His table, but few to take part in His fasting. All desire to be happy with Him; few wish to suffer anything for Him. Many follow Him to the breaking of bread, but few to the drinking of the chalice of His passion. Many revere His miracles; few approach the shame of the Cross. Many love Him as long as they encounter no hardship; many praise and bless him as long as they receive some comfort from Him. But if Jesus hides Himself and leaves them for a while, they fall either into complaints or into deep dejection. Those, on the contrary, who love Him for His own sake and not for any comfort of their own, bless Him in all trial and anguish of heart as well as in the bliss of consolation. Even if He should never give them consolation, yet they would continue to praise Him and wish always to give Him thanks. What power there is in pure love for Jesus—love that is free from all self-interest and self-love!"[13]

The sacrifice of Christ in death on the cross is not merely the starting point of the Christian life. It is the experience that determines the balance of our lives in Christ. When we get into Jesus' life, we enter into His death. The nature of His death is stamped on our hearts. Christ's death was a denial of Himself. The mark of His cross on our lives is self-denial. Christ's death was with reference to sin. The mark of the cross embossed on our lives is our dying to sin. Christ's death provided the painful portal through which we pass from death (the consequence of our own self-styled rebellion) to life, and that, eternal. In other words, when, by faith, I get into Jesus' life and enter into His death, I recognize that with Him I vicariously experience death with reference to the person I was before I was joined to Him by faith. Dying with Christ breaks the continuity of my life in Christ now from my life apart from Christ when I was "dead in trespasses and sins," and enslaved to my selfish sin nature. Passing through death, Christ was raised triumphantly from the dead by the power of the Father. By that same power, I, who have died with Christ, am raised to *live in newness of life* (Romans 6:4). For the Christian who has been raised with Christ by the power of the Holy Spirit, newness of life is more than an idea or concept. It becomes our life experience. That is why the Bible makes such an issue about the incongruity of ongoing sin patterns in a Christian's life when he has died with Jesus in reference to that sin and has embraced new life in Christ. As Scripture asks so emphatically, *"How can we who died to sin, still live in it?"* (Romans 6:2.) In Christ's life, I am a man made new.

The Apostle Paul explains the impact and implications of this profound experience called newness of life attained by entering into Christ's death and resurrection.

"The love of Christ controls us, because we have concluded this: that one has died for all, therefore all have died; and he died for all, that those who live

might no longer live for themselves but for him who for their sakes died and was raised. From now on, therefore, we regard no one according to the flesh. Even though we once regarded Christ according to the flesh, we regard him thus no longer. Therefore, if anyone is in Christ, he is a new creation. The old has passed away; behold, the new has come. All this is from God, who through Christ has reconciled us to himself...." (2 Corinthians 5:14-17.)

In Christ, I am a new creation. The homely caterpillar is being transformed into a beautiful butterfly. As a new creation, I have the possibility of a new perspective—how I view myself, others, and Christ. The fundamental change that God affects within me when I get into Jesus' life determines how I come at my personal life, how I relate to others, and how I respond to Jesus. It addresses the very thing Jesus asked me to deny—myself—by moving me to live no longer for myself but for him who for my sake died and was raised again. My standards, values, goals, orientations, ethics, relationships, and everything else change. The cross of Christ marks all of life as we enter into His death and glorious resurrection. The byword of my life is no longer "my will be done," but "Thy will be done," that self-denying, God-embracing attitude Jesus displayed in the garden of his deepest sorrow as he faced the horror of crucifixion on a Roman cross for our sakes. The vast possibilities that are open to me by entering into Christ's death and resurrection become my experience as I act on their veracity. The sixth chapter of *Romans* holds the key. I invite you to pause here and read that entire chapter.

Once a person begins to comprehend the enormity of God's love for him and grace to him in Christ, he may be tempted to exploit that love or cheapen that grace by taking advantage of both through careless and spiritually undisciplined living. This is evidenced by the immorality, divorce, dabbling in pornography, embracing "alternative lifestyles," anger, unforgiving attitudes and scandalous behavior of all kinds rampant among professing Christians and even Christian leaders, along with the neglect of truthfulness, integrity, compassion, generosity, love and unity. Getting into Jesus' life by entering into his death and resurrection will remedy that. Because my death to sin and resurrection to newness of life have taken place vicariously in Christ, I am no longer bound to the self-absorbed nature to which I was previously chained. I can, in fact, consider myself dead to the temptations and sins that once held me. This will allow me to choose obedience to Christ rather than to sin. The Apostle Paul details this when he says, *"The death he [Christ] died he died to sin, once for all, but the life he lives he lives to God. So you also must consider yourselves dead to sin and alive to God in Christ Jesus. Let not sin therefore reign in your mortal bodies, to make you obey their passions. Do not present your members to sin as instruments for unrighteousness, but present yourselves to God as those who have been brought from death to life, and your members to God as instruments for righteousness. For sin will have no dominion over you…"* (Romans 6:11-14a). This is undoubtedly what Jesus had in mind when he called us to "take up our cross daily." In doing so, we consider ourselves as good as dead toward sin, but very alive to God. Such a consideration comes from an understanding of what people contemporary to Jesus associated with the cross.

In the days of the Roman Empire, the criminally condemned carried their crosses to the site of their crucifixion. The cross on their shoulders signified that they were as good as dead. They were dead men walking. When Jesus invited us into His life with the words "If any man will come after me, let him deny himself, *take up his cross daily*, and follow me," he undoubtedly had in mind the idea that a person taking up a cross was as good as dead, his crucifixion being certain. Therefore, Jesus could use that analogy to signify the spiritual reckoning that I must do as a Christian. When I take up that cross each day, I intentionally consider my former self apart from Christ as good as dead—I am a dead man walking. We cannot follow Christ without this death. But my reckoning doesn't stop there. Because my renewed self is raised with Christ to newness of life, I can actually present myself as alive to God and the members of my body (my faculties and body parts) as tools for the practice and perpetuation of righteousness—those attitudes and actions that are in harmony with God's pure moral character and that reflect love for God and neighbor. What a glorious picture! Nevertheless, Christians often live in perpetual spiritual defeat, giving in to the pull of their sinful natures rather than experiencing the victory secured for them by Christ's death and resurrection and appropriating that victory. Why do you suppose that is true? Don't they know that a change has taken place?

Recently, I had occasion to ride the red line elevated train into Chicago where I witnessed a curious and saddening event. All the seats on the train were occupied when a new batch of passengers got on. Immediately, at the back of the car in which I was riding, an elderly black woman got out of her seat to make it available to the younger white passengers who were boarding. She could hardly stand, but she got up anyway. Why do you suppose she did that? Could it be that she was still living on the basis of past codes and experiences? Had she lived in a part of the country where she would not only be expected to vacate her seat, but coerced to do so? Didn't she know that her situation had changed and that she now had the freedom to retain her seat on that train? Yet, she was presenting herself for obedience to a master who no longer had that kind of clout in her life.

An elephant on the circus grounds can often be contained by a chain around one leg connected to a small stake in the ground. This has always perplexed me. Why doesn't the elephant realize that it could easily uproot that stake and walk away to freedom? One day I learned that it has to do with its previous capture and containment. The elephant would be lured into a trap that would ensnare one of its legs. The snare was secured to a banyan tree whose deep roots and unusual strength made it impossible for the elephant's escape, try as it may through pulling, pushing, and butting, to free itself. Once the elephant is convinced that he cannot overcome the snare that holds him, he can be secured to a small stake. Even though he has been set free from the banyan tree and could easily overcome the stake that now holds him, the familiarity of his previous condition persuades him that he must submit to his captivity. How foolish and fearful, we say, of that elderly woman to surrender her seat. How ignorant of the elephant to submit to that deceitful tether. Yet, how are these different from Christians who have been set free from the reign of sin in their lives by the death and resurrection of their Savior, but continue to live in sin as though they have no other choice? Do we not realize that by getting into Jesus' life and entering into his death and resurrection, we can experience new possibilities?

After quoting Romans 6:14, *"For sin shall not have dominion over you, for you are not under the law, but under grace,"* Martyn Lloyd-Jones urges, "Oh, that men and women might understand what that means. You know, people will think of Christianity as just that which offers pardon for our sin, that God says: 'Very well, I forgive,' but that then you remain exactly where you were, and you go back into the same old world with your same old weakness. And there you are as you always were, and you fail and you sin again, and you ask forgiveness again, and up and down you go, back and forth, and you are exactly the same, except that now God forgives you....But that is not Christianity. That may be the beginning of it...but it is nothing but the beginning. This is the essential thing—that my whole position is changed; my whole relationship to God is changed. I am not only at peace with him, I am in an entirely new relationship. This is the difference."[14]

It's time for an honest confession. For years I studied the life and ministry of Jesus, both formally and informally. I stood in awe of His mercy, grace and self-giving love. I read with wonder the Bible's descriptions of the possibility of a transformed life that is being shaped into the likeness of Jesus. With excitement and enthusiasm I taught others about this possibility. As I envisioned the prospects of the genuine Christian life, my soul soared as one's heart is lifted by the radiant beauty of a glorious multi-chromatic sunset. But to a point, I was only an enthusiastic observer instead of a self-denying participant. I avoided the radical nature of the mark of Christ's cross on my own life. Unfortunately, I was not alone within the Christian community. Nor would I be today. Yet, as God's Spirit nagged me with the very Scriptures I was teaching to others, I began to realize that I was missing a vital and necessary dimension of my faith in Christ, the purpose for which Christ saved me—life transformation, the restoration of the image of God in me. And I recognized that as the non-Christian world observes Christians in this condition, it does not see the reality of the crucified, yet risen Christ vibrant within the people who say they are His followers. It occurred to me that we Christians must not merely talk or teach or sing about Christ's death and resurrection as theological certainties. We must enter into these as life-changing realities—whatever it takes.

The single-minded focus of the Apostle Paul and countless other of our forbears of faith in Jesus Christ was to experience the life-changing reality of entering into and sharing in the death and resurrection of Jesus. Listen to how Paul expresses it in Philippians 3: 8-14:

"I count all things as loss in view of the surpassing value of knowing Christ Jesus my Lord, for whom I have suffered the loss of all things, and count them but rubbish in order that I might gain Christ, and may be found in Him, not having a righteousness of my own derived from the Law, but that which is through faith in Christ, the righteousness which comes from God on the basis of faith; that I may know Him, and the power of His resurrection and the fellowship of His sufferings, being conformed to His death, in order that I may attain to the resurrection from the dead. Not that I have already obtained it, or have already become perfect, but I press on in order that I may lay hold of that for which also I was laid hold of by Christ Jesus.... Forgetting what is past and reaching forward to what is ahead, I press on toward the goal for the prize of the upward call of God in Christ Jesus."

There is immeasurable value in knowing Christ experientially and sharing in His death and the power of His resurrection albeit vicariously. We can share in the sufferings of Christ's self-sacrificing death when we give up those things that violate our relationship with Him and as we live in harmony with His will as His representatives in a fallen and corrupt world. The ability to do this comes from the power of Christ's resurrection now, and the promise of our being resurrected one day when Christ comes again.

The latter is the "upward call" of which Paul writes in Philippians 3. Paul focused on the value of knowing Christ experientially by sharing in his death and resurrection in order to realize first hand the purposes for which Christ had "laid hold" of him. To do this, he put aside the pride of past successes *and* the self-deprecation of past failures, including the persecution and killing of Christians. Remember that prior to becoming a Christian, Paul was a bright and self-righteous religious leader passionately opposed to this new movement called Christianity—fervent to the point of leading the charge to stop the movement and stamp out its adherents. Only death to that past and the renewal of resurrection power could free him from the potential pathology that might result from such deeds. He set his sights solely on Jesus. That changed everything—liberating him from his painful past. It changed his priorities, from the self-sufficiency that depended on religious status and being a "do-gooder," to pursuit of knowing Christ personally and gaining Christ experientially. It changed his character because he received the righteousness that God gave to him through faith in Jesus Christ and no longer depended on a self-righteousness shaped by his own self-efforts. And it changed his destiny. Through the power of Christ's resurrection, he would also be raised from the dead, be called upward to heaven, and enjoy citizenship there with a body that has been completely transformed (Philippians 3:11-21).

We who may be so much like this Apostle before his conversion, who rely on our religious affiliations and our relatively good deeds to gain acceptance with

God, while desperately needing to be set free from a painful past, we too are in need of the same transformation from the inside out. But now, entering into Christ's death and resurrection affects us in every way. Now the choices we make and the actions we take are determined by new priorities, changed character, and a glorious destiny.

When we get into Jesus' life, that union not only changes us and how we view ourselves and others, but also how God sees us. When God looks at our past He sees a death on the cross, for we have died with His Son. He credits us with that death which secures for us His pardon for our sin. When God looks at our present, He sees the resurrected life of His Son shining in us for we have been raised with Christ and credited with His perfect life. Now God encourages us to behavior that matches what He already sees. When God looks at our future, He sees us glorified and seated with His Son in heaven, reveling in radiant joy. Knowing this, we realize that there is no need for us to try to get God to like us or accept us. He sees our lives are hidden in Christ's life (Colossians 3:3). He loves us immeasurably, and accepts us as we are. His love and grace become the purest motivations for our holiness and our desire to please Him.

I deeply appreciated a letter Brennan Manning included in his book *The Signature of Jesus.* The letter was found in the office of a young pastor in Zimbabwe, Africa shortly after he had been martyred for his faith in Jesus Christ. He wrote:

"I'm part of the fellowship of the unashamed. I have the Holy Spirit power. The die has been cast.

I have stepped over the line. The decision has been made—I'm a disciple of His. I won't look back, let up, slow down, back away, or be still. My past is redeemed, my present makes sense, my future is secure. I'm finished and done with low living, sight walking, smooth knees, colorless dreams, tamed visions, worldly talking, cheap giving, and dwarfed goals.

I no longer need preeminence, prosperity, position, promotions, plaudits, or popularity. I don't have to be right, first, tops, recognized, praised, regarded, or rewarded. I now live by faith, lean on his presence, walk by patience, am uplifted by prayer, and labor with power.

My face is set, my gait is fast, my goal is heaven, my road is narrow, my way rough, my companions are few, my Guide reliable, my mission clear. I cannot be bought, compromised, detoured, lured away, turned back, deluded, or delayed. I will not flinch in the face of sacrifice, hesitate in the presence of the enemy, pander at the pool of popularity, or meander in the maze of mediocrity.

I won't give up, shut up, let up, until I have stayed up, stored up, prayed up, paid up, preached up for the cause of Christ. I am a disciple of Jesus. I must go till he comes, give till I drop, preach till all know, and work till he stops me. And, when he comes for his own, he will have no problem recognizing me...my banner is clear!"[15]

Clearly, this is the testimony of someone who has entered into Jesus' death and resurrection, and is no longer living for himself, but for Him who died and was raised again for his sake. The question I must ask myself (I invite you to ask it of yourself as well) is, does this in any way describe me?

To enter into Jesus' death is to respond positively to His insight: "He who loses his life for my sake and the Gospel's, shall find it!" (Mark 8:35.) Such dying consists in surrender. Jesus does not want us merely to attempt to live for him the best we can. Just as Christ loved us and gave Himself up for us, He wants us to love Him in self-denying surrender so that he can live his risen life in and through us. As the Apostle Paul asserts passionately, "I have been crucified with Christ. Nevertheless, I live. Yet, it is not I who live, but Christ who lives in me. And the life I now live, I live by faith in the Son of God who loved me and gave himself up for me" (Galatians 2:20).

Getting into Jesus life and trusting him with abandon, we enter into his self-denying death, only to find ourselves emerging from death to newness of life as we attach ourselves to a risen and reigning Savior. Risen with Christ, we set our minds on and seek the eternal things which are above, where Christ is, and do not allow ourselves to be preoccupied with temporal things on earth (Colossians 3:1-3). Our overriding life goal is to be Christ-centered, our life-purposes driven by His purposes, His will and His values. The words of the hymn writer Daniel W. Whittle become the theme of our song: *"Dying with Jesus, by death reckoned mine; living with Jesus a new life divine. Looking to Jesus 'til glory doth shine; Moment by moment, O Lord, I am Thine."*

CHAPTER SIX:

LETTING CHRIST HEAL YOUR PAINFUL PAST

Jennifer woke up with a start. Was that the slamming of a door? She rolled over to find the space next to her in the bed still warm, but empty. Where had he gone? What about the promises he made the night before that convinced her to let him spend the night? One week later she still had not heard from him. A sick, empty feeling gripped her. How could she have been so foolish? Everything her parents had taught her, every caution they had given her came rushing back. She began to wonder if the commitment she had made to Jesus Christ was even valid. After all, wasn't what she had done a major sin? Two months later her pregnancy with the child conceived of an impetuous, but foolish choice was confirmed. Panic set in. A friend directed her to a clinic that would relieve her of this burden. Yet, after the abortion, her guilt only grew, the wounds deepened, and doubts about her worthiness even to call herself a Christian increased. How would she ever experience relief from this painful past? Was healing even possible? Jesus answers, "Yes!"

As we have just seen, entering into Jesus death and resurrection means "dying" to a former way of life and embracing the new life to which He is calling us, "forgetting the past and pressing on to that which lies ahead" as the Apostle Paul describes in Philippians 3:13, 14. But here is where so many of us get stuck. We can't let go of the past. Or, to put it another way, the past won't let go of us. Things that have happened to us or things we have done in the past immobilize us, impeding our progress into the relationship with Christ that we've been considering and for which we are longing. We need to know that Jesus understands, not simply cognitively, but experientially. We need to know that Christ can heal that painful past.

I was just eight years old when my two-year-old brother went missing. We looked all over for him. Neighbors joined the search for hours. Nothing. Night was falling. In exasperation, my father turned to me and said, "John, you were supposed to be watching your brother. If anything has happened to him, it's your fault." Needless to say, his words cut deeply into my childish heart. That was a huge burden for an eight-year-old to bear. Shortly after that, we found my brother, safe and sound. But I have thought often of the devastating pain that would have been mine had my brother been seriously hurt or killed. And even though the worst did not happen, the fact that my father felt the way he did and said those painful words to me stayed with me for a long time.

Often, memories of broken dreams and hurts from the past haunt us and keep us from responding to God's love and to Christ's call to get into His life and follow Him. Some time ago, I listened to a young woman who wept convulsively as she told me about her sexual abuse at the hands of her father. When the abuse started, she was too young to know what was happening. Soon the abuse was a pattern. As she grew older, she knew it was wrong, but she felt trapped and that somehow she was to blame. She became emotionally confused. She took onto herself the shame that belonged to her father. Tragically, she allowed that shame to drive her toward promiscuous sexual behavior so that her pain was compounded by the guilt of her own wrongdoing. Deep within herself, she felt unworthy even to pray to—much less to follow—Christ or call herself a Christian.

Yes, many times our families are the source of past pain. Sometimes, we carry pain from places other than our families—a friend who betrayed us, a financial reversal, a failed opportunity. Perhaps we loved someone who did not love us in return. These things and more can bring the inner pain that challenges our faith.

The same is true within the church community. Often members inflict pain on one another. Sometimes a church leader fails and a whole congregation feels hurt or betrayed. God wants us to get past that because He knows what harboring such pain can do to us. He also knows that we will even use such things as excuses for mediocrity in our Christian living and service. God understands that a painful past can foster anger, resentment or bitterness in us, giving Satan a foothold in our lives (Ephesians 4:26, 27). That is why God wants us to confront the pain of our past, hear Jesus say, "I understand," and let Him forgive us, heal us and restore us to wholeness.

If anyone had reason to harbor bitterness because of pain inflicted upon him by others, it is that Old Testament "Christ-type" Joseph, whose unrelenting faith in God foreshadowed the flint-hard resolve of Jesus Himself. Wounded and betrayed by jealous brothers, enslaved by traveling merchants, forgotten by people he had helped, and falsely accused after refusing to engage in a sexual affair with his employer's seductive wife, Joseph found comfort, healing and the ability to forgive in the presence of the Lord he loved. After God came to his rescue and prospered him, he found himself in a position to wreak revenge on the brothers who started all his troubles. But instead, because of the grace he had received from the Lord, he was able to say to them, "As for you, you meant evil against me, but God meant it for good in order to bring about the present results" (Genesis 50:20).

Think of Stephen, that early follower of Jesus who, because of his faith, was stoned to death by his detractors. As the skull-splitting pain of rocks hurled in anger unjustly pounded the life from his body, he found grace from his Lord to utter the very words Jesus Himself had cried from the cross, "Father, forgive them!" As he looked heavenward and caught an early glimpse of his Savior, he knew that Jesus understands. As a result, he was able to look beyond his personal pain and beyond the faults of the very people inflicting it, to see their need and pray for their forgiveness. That same grace is available to us.

I found that grace when reading Ephesians 4:32, "Be kind to one another, tenderhearted, forgiving each other, just as God in Christ has forgiven you." Suddenly I was struck with the realization that just as I had been forgiven because of Christ's amazing grace, unconditional love, and sacrificial payment for my sin on the cross, I needed to extend that same mercy and forgiveness toward those who had wounded me. The wounds from my father sprang to my mind. Yet, my father was deceased. How would this happen? I found a quiet place where I could be alone with the Lord and my own thoughts. There, in my mind's eye, I saw myself with my father in Jesus' presence. I imagined what Jesus would say, "John, I understand the pain you feel. I know what wounds feel like. But by my wounds, you have been forgiven. It's time for you to extend that same forgiveness to your Dad." Indeed it was. I turned and said, "Dad, I forgive you. I love you. Jesus understands, and now I do as well." I cannot describe how exuberant I felt to be a conduit of the very grace I had received from my Savior.

Sometimes our pain comes from our own choices. A son rebels against his parents, saying and doing hurtful things; a girl runs away from home; a man cheats on his wife or steals from his company; a father or mother laments the time they did *not* give to their now-grown children. The list goes on. You could add to that list your own painful past experiences.

However, if we are going to fully discover God's plans for us and make them our own, it is crucial that we deal with that painful past, whatever it is, and let Christ forgive and heal it so that we can let it go.

I have experienced such pain from my past, not only because of things done to me by someone else, but because of choices I made which I knew were wrong but I did anyway—bringing me shame and guilt. Had I not discovered how to let go of a painful past through Christ's understanding, forgiveness and healing touch, I could easily be stuck in the past without hope and without dreams.

The Bible holds many illustrations of how real people dealt with past personal pain they experienced because of choices they made. Some may have made these choices because of hurt inflicted upon them by someone else. By considering a few well-known characters, we can gain insight that will help us realize how well Jesus understands our predicament and how He can help us deal with our own painful pasts. The first example is found in the Old Testament, in 2 Samuel 11:1-12:13. You may want to take a moment to read the account.

King David of Israel: A Past of Adultery, Murder and Deceit

It is incongruous that a man with King David's stature, integrity, success and nobility could weave the web he did. But there he was, in what we might call a "mid-life crisis." He had stayed home from the battle in which his armies were engaged. He had time on his hands as he strolled on the terrace roof of the palace. From that vantage point, his gaze fell on the beautiful Bathsheba, bathing in her own residence. Lust sprang up in David's heart. His mind played with the possibilities. And he gave in to the destructive temptation. Using his position of authority, and knowing that her husband was away with the army, he sent for Bathsheba. When she came to him, he seduced her, had sexual relations with her and sent her back home. Then came the bad news—Bathsheba was pregnant as a result of those relations. For David, cover up was among the alternatives he had, and the one he chose. One bad choice led to another. He called Bathsheba's husband, Uriah, home from the battlefield so that Uriah would have sexual relations with his wife and be credited for the pregnancy. David would be in the clear. But Uriah was of nobler stock and refused the pleasures of the home front while his comrades were engaged in the battle. David began to panic and took further measures to hide his sin. He had dinner with Uriah and gave him a lot of wine in an attempt to get him drunk. Perhaps then Uriah would let down his guard and sleep with his wife. But Uriah slept it off away from his house. The only recourse David felt he had left was to have Uriah killed. David arranged this by having Uriah placed at the front of the battle lines in the most vulnerable place possible. His strategy worked. Uriah died in the battle. Immorality, deceit, lies, and murder now stained David's heart. The pain that accompanied these would undermine David's relationship with God until a prophet named Nathan confronted David about his sins, and moved David to repentance.

David's actions affected Bathsheba, her husband, David's family, the child that was born, and ultimately, the entire nation. When writing about this later, David says in Psalm 32:3, "When I kept silent about my sin, I wasted away, groaning all day long. My vitality was drained." At first, David dealt with the pain and shame of his past like so many of us deal with ours—he denied it. Shame does not like to be confronted. Shame and guilt will push us toward denial of the pain we feel. Soon we become skilled at denial and end up with an unacknowledged list of issues we won't face. This will wear us down and will keep us from the only relationship that can bring full healing and restoration. There is significant irony here: our fear of the unavoidable discomfort in addressing our own sin and painful past keeps us in a perpetual state of unresolved guilt and pain. Until we confront and deal with the painful issues from our past, we will feel estranged from God, we will never get relief, and we will never be healed. David experienced that as he denied his painful past. But then he writes in Psalm 32:5, "I acknowledged my sin to you, O God. My guilt I did not hide. I said, 'I will confess my transgressions to the Lord.' And you forgave the guilt of my sin." David was refreshed. His vitality returned. So did the vibrancy of his relationship with God and the realization of God's plans for him.

As I've already indicated, David did get a little help coming to grips with his past. He denied as long as he could, in spite of the pain. But then he was confronted by the prophet Nathan. Perhaps the Lord would use our discussion in this chapter to move you to confront pain from your past so that you can experience Christ's healing and the refreshment of His understanding and forgiveness—the kind that enabled David to finish Psalm 32 with these words, *"You forgave the guilt of my sin. Therefore, let everyone who is godly pray to You in a time when You may be found… You are my hiding place; You preserve me from trouble and surround me with songs of deliverance…Many are the sorrows of the wicked, but he who trusts in the Lord, mercy and love will surround him."*

The next illustration comes from the life of a man very close to Jesus,

The Apostle Peter: A Past of Self-Assertion and Outright Denial of Jesus Christ

Peter's troubles started when, in pursuit of his own interests rather than God's, he began to take life's matters into his own hands. As we saw earlier, when Jesus discussed the necessity of His own suffering and crucifixion as part and parcel of God's plan, Peter rebuked Jesus and tried to coerce him out of such talk. When Jesus was arrested in the Garden of Gethsemane, Peter pulled a sword and unsuccessfully tried to prevent the arrest that would lead Jesus to the cross. Then, totally frustrated and disillusioned, and even though he had sworn undying allegiance to Jesus, Peter vehemently denied any association with his Master, not once, not twice, but three times, couching the denials in cursing and vile epithets. Almost immediately, the pain of what he had done cut him deeply. He ran off and wept bitterly. Then, from a distance, he watched the tragic death of his dearest friend. Peter was the despairing survivor of a broken cause and shattered dreams.

Imagine the paralyzing self-loathing with which Peter must have lived during those long days following Jesus' crucifixion. He who had previously left his life and livelihood to help build a kingdom, who had insisted that he would never fail Jesus no matter what the circumstances, could not stand in the moment when his loyalty would have been most valued. And with Jesus now dead, Peter had no opportunity to rectify the situation even if he had had the emotional fortitude to do so. Dejected, Peter returned to his daily work. Devastated by the irreversible wrong he had committed, he would endure the pain, but he would never dream again.

Yet, Peter was in for a shock. On Easter Sunday he got the word—Jesus' tomb was empty! Christ had broken the bonds of guilt and shame and death. He was alive, bringing hope to every person with a painful past. It is important to note, however, that while forgiveness had been secured through Christ's death and resurrection, the process by which Peter could and would be healed, restored and released from his sin and the powerful memories of it was not completed. In fact, it had yet to be experienced.

On a quiet beach along the Sea of Galilee, where the risen Jesus prepared and ate breakfast with His amazed and bewildered followers, Jesus confronts Peter with the reality of Peter's painful past and the choices he had made. Then, Jesus gives Peter a new beginning, a chance to be forgiven, restored and set free from the past that plagued him. John 21:15-17, lets us eaves drop on their interchange: "When they had finished breakfast, Jesus said to Simon Peter, 'Simon, son of John, do you love me more than these?' Peter said to Him, 'Yes, Lord, You know that I love you.' Jesus said to him, 'Tend my sheep.' Jesus said to Peter again a second time, 'Simon, son of John, do you love me?' Peter said to Him, 'Yes, Lord, You know that I love you.' Jesus said to him, 'Shepherd my sheep.' Jesus said to Peter a third time, 'Simon, son of John, do you love me?' Peter was grieved because Jesus said to him the third time, 'Do you love me?' And Peter said to him, 'Lord, you know all things. You know that I love you.' Jesus said to him, 'Tend my sheep.'"

Can you see what Jesus does? As though undoing Peter's past failures and three denials, Jesus asks him three times, "Peter, do you love Me?" Jesus is giving to Peter (and to us) a specific pathway to forgiveness and healing—to face up to the reality of the pain and its cause, and then to surrender himself to the Lord in love. In so many words, Jesus says to Peter, "The issue isn't that you failed. We all know you blew it. The question is where do we go from here? Peter, do YOU *love* ME?" This was neither an easy or pleasant experience for Peter. As we saw earlier, Scripture says, "Peter was *grieved* because Jesus said to him the third time, 'Do you love me?'" And Jesus is not asking the question three times merely to say, "You failed three times, so you owe three apologies." Rather, it is as if each time Christ asks this of Peter, he brings Peter more fully into the reality of his failure and the magnitude of the forgiveness and deliverance Jesus is offering. Each time Peter affirmed his love for Jesus, he surrendered his past and his pain to his Lord. Each time the Lord gave him the next step—serve me, tend my sheep, follow me. Such invitations from Jesus can mean only one thing—that Jesus had forgiven Peter his painful past and was willing to use Peter in his service. Christ released Peter from past failure. All Peter needed to do now was to accept Christ's acceptance of him and to forgive himself. In doing so, he could freely enjoy the relationship with Jesus that would transform his life. Notice too that Jesus urges Peter to respond with full and complete Christian service.

But what about us? Isn't it true that often we don't engage in this transforming process and receive the restoration Jesus offers because the process is so uncomfortable in and of itself? Yet, there is a dangerous irony here. In avoiding the pain of confronting our sins and experiencing Jesus' understanding, forgiveness and acceptance, we imprison ourselves indefinitely in a painful past that is infinitely more uncomfortable and debilitating. There is a better way. Like Peter, we must bow in the presence of Jesus and let him fully confront the reality of our past choices and sins, respond to Him with our own affirmations of love and commitment, accept His forgiveness and His acceptance of us and say "yes" to His invitation to embark on a life of usefulness and significance. You see, negative patterns precipitated by the past must be replaced by positive actions for the future. It is God's way of showing us we have a future in His plans for us if we will let Him set us free from what has held us hostage and is causing us pain. No one learned that better than

The Apostle Paul: A Past of Treachery, Persecution and Killing of Christians

Imagine the baggage Paul carried as a Christian. Many of us cringe at the thought of particularly hurtful or shameful things we've said or done—even as children or adolescents. Yet, Paul had spent years prior to his conversion to Christ hunting down, persecuting and even executing Christians. Few of us own guilt of this magnitude. And to be sure, there were numerous early Christians who were skeptical of Paul's conversion and more than willing to remind him regularly of his past treachery. Paul had a very painful past. Undoubtedly, his dreams at night were filled with the screams of those he tortured for their faith. How could he ever forget or escape the pain of what he had done?

The answer to that question is in his single-minded desire to experience the life-changing reality of vicariously entering into and sharing in the death and resurrection of Jesus. He explains this in Philippians 3:8-13: "I count all things as loss in view of the surpassing value of knowing Christ Jesus my Lord, for whom I have suffered the loss of all things, and count them but rubbish in order that I might gain Christ, and may be found in Him, not having a righteousness of my own derived from the Law, but that which is through faith in Christ, the righteousness which comes from God on the basis of faith; that I may know Him, and the power of His resurrection

and the fellowship of His sufferings, being conformed to His death, in order that I may attain to the
resurrection from the dead. Not that I have already
obtained it, or have already become perfect, but I
press on in order that I may lay hold of that for which
also I was laid hold of by Christ Jesus."

In his mind and in his heart, Paul knelt before
the cross of Christ and saw Christ dying there for
his (Paul's) sins, his wounds, his painful past. But
he was also able to see something more—that in
coming to Christ by faith he was united to Christ.
Consequently, Paul saw *Paul with the painful past*
hanging and dying there with Jesus. Paul with the
painful past, together with every treacherous thing
he had done and every hurt he suffered or inflicted,
died there on that cross with Christ. His past was
gone in that death. But he did not stop and stay
there. Paul also understood that he was resurrected
with Christ to newness of life. He no longer had his
own past, but Christ's. That is why he wrote to the
Christians in Galatia, "I am crucified with Christ.
It is no longer I who live, but Christ lives in me;
and the life which I now live in the flesh I live by
faith in the Son of God, who loved me, and gave
Himself up for me" (Galatians 2:20).

There is immeasurable value in knowing Christ
experientially and sharing in His death and the power
of His resurrection albeit vicariously. We can experience the deliverance from a painful past and the
blessed hope of a positive future in this relationship to Christ. The ability to do this comes from the
power of Christ's resurrection now, and the promise

of our being resurrected one day when Christ comes again. The latter is the "upward call" of which Paul writes in Philippians 3. Paul focused on the value of knowing Christ experientially by sharing in his death and resurrection in order to realize first hand the purposes for which Christ had "laid hold" of him. To do this, he put aside the pride of past successes and the self-deprecation of past failures, including the persecution and killing of Christians. Only *death* to that past and the renewal of resurrection power he experienced within could free him from the potential pathology that might result from such deeds. He brought His pain to Jesus. He set his sights solely on Jesus. That changed everything. It did away with his past. It changed his priorities, from the self-sufficiency that depended on religious status and being a "do-gooder," to pursuit of knowing Christ personally and gaining Christ experientially. It changed his character because he received the righteousness that God gave to him through faith in Jesus Christ and not a self-righteousness shaped by his own self-efforts. And it changed his destiny. Through the power of Christ's resurrection, he would also be raised from the dead, be called upward to heaven, and enjoy citizenship there with a body that has been completely transformed (Philippians 3:11-21). No wonder Paul preaches to the Christians in Corinth, "If any person is in Christ, he is a new creation. The old has passed away. The new has come" (2 Corinthians 5:17).

It is not surprising then that Paul's summary comment in Philippians 3:14 is, "Forgetting what is past and reaching forward to what is ahead, I press

on toward the goal for the prize of the upward call of
God in Christ Jesus." Bringing us to

YOU AND ME: A Past That Surfaces in Our Memories, Needing Christ's Forgiveness and Healing

By now, things from your own past may have sur-
faced. All too often, people who have decided to follow
Jesus, have come to him for a kind of generic forgiveness
of all their sins without bringing to him specific past sins
that still haunt them, or the pain of hurt or abuse inflicted
on them by others. As a result, they don't experience
the forgiveness and healing that refreshes and renews.
As I looked at the profound forgiveness and remarkable
deliverance from painful pasts for these people, David,
Peter and Paul, I thought of how God had done similar
things for me where I have failed him with the choices
I've made; where I have hurt others with my words or
actions, or where I was wounded by the words or actions
of others. I am in awe of the amazing grace and love of
our Lord Jesus. Yet, this is precisely what Jesus said He
would do in people's lives when, at the outset of His
ministry, He read these prophetic words from Isaiah
61 to describe His mission, "The Spirit of the Lord is
upon me, because He anointed me to preach the Gospel
to the poor, He has sent me to proclaim release to the
captives and recovery of sight to the blind, to set free
those who are oppressed." Jesus will forgive, heal and
set free, those who are bound, blinded and oppressed by
their painful pasts. Isaiah 61:3 describes the results: *"To
those who mourn…I will give a crown of beauty instead*

of ashes, the oil of gladness instead of mourning, the garment of praise instead of a spirit of despair."

It isn't as if Jesus doesn't understand a painful past, or doesn't know how to deal with it. He was misunderstood by His family, abused by religious leaders, betrayed by a close associate, denied by a dear friend, and abandoned by almost everybody else. As He writhed on the cross bearing all the agony of our sins and pain, He felt forsaken by His Heavenly Father in His hour of greatest need. He was wounded wrongly because of our sins. He suffered for our guilt. But He didn't hold on to any of it. From the cross of His suffering He prayed these words, "Father, forgive them..." In His resurrection from the dead, Jesus brings us hope, not just a generic forgiveness by which we can gain access to heaven, but a repairing process that deals with our individual and specific areas of paralyzing pain. His specialty is healing damaged people, mending broken lives, restoring us to dare to dream again. This is the description of Jesus in Hebrews 4:15, 16: *"We do not have a high priest who cannot sympathize with our weaknesses, but One [Jesus, the Son of God] who has been tempted in all things as we are, yet without sin. Therefore let us draw near with confidence to the throne of grace, so that we may receive mercy and find grace to help in time of need."*

Isn't this the person you would want to turn to, to heal your painful past? If you were going to build a house, would you go to a lifetime apartment dweller for information and advice? No, you would seek out people who have been through the experience of building a new house. I have an earned doctor's degree. But if you were going to have surgery, you wouldn't ask Dr. Vosnos to do it, would you? My training and experience is in a totally different field. You would want a surgeon who has experience doing your kind of surgery. You would also find yourself talking to people who have been through your kind of surgery. You want people who are qualified to discuss the matter and help you go through it.

Someone once said, "You may soon forget those with whom you have laughed, but you will never forget those with whom you have wept." Author Henri Nouwen reminds us that "when we honestly ask ourselves which person in our lives means the most to us, we often find that it is those who . . . have chosen . . . to share our pain and touch our wounds with a gentle and tender hand."[16]

To whom do you go when you are dealing with the trials in your life, temptations to sin, personal suffering, fears, or even death? To whom do you turn when experiencing the phobias that keep you from reaching out to others in love with the Gospel of Jesus, fears of feeling foolish, being rejected or simply failing? Do you want somebody who can identify with all of these things? There is such a Person. The Bible calls Him a friend that sticks closer than a brother. He is Jesus, our great Savior. Jesus understands—qualifying Him to come to our aid.

Jesus Understands Because He Moved into Our Neighborhood, Becoming Like Us

"Therefore, because the children [of God] have flesh and blood, he [Jesus] too shared in their humanity so that by his death he might destroy him who holds the power of death—that is, the devil—and free those who all their lives were held in slavery by their fear of death...For this reason he had to be made like his brothers in every way, in order that he might become a merciful and faithful high priest in service to God, and that he might make atonement for the sins of the people. Because he himself suffered when he was tempted, he is able help those who are being tempted." (Hebrews 2:14-18 NIV).

The Bible tells us here and in several other places that Jesus, the Son of God, left His heavenly glory and moved right into our neighborhood. When He did, He came with nothing more than any of us has and a lot less than most of us have. There are two themes that thread their way through this passage, *incarnation* and *suffering* and how, by these, Jesus achieved a close relationship between Himself and mankind, and more specifically, between Himself and those of us who put our faith in Him and become fully pardoned children of God. Consequently, through His incarnation and subsequent suffering, the following things are true: *a) he brings us to glory; b) he is not ashamed to call us family; c) he has shared our common experience of life in a fallen and corrupt world; d) he became like us—flesh and blood; and e) he can give us help.*

The first theme is *incarnation*. We find the Bible describing it in John 1:14 as "the Word [God] became flesh and lived among us." Or in Philippians 2:5ff., "Christ Jesus, Who, being in very nature God, did not consider equality with God something to be grasped, but made himself nothing, taking the very nature of a servant, being made in human likeness. And being found in appearance as a man, he humbled himself and became obedient to death—even death on a cross!" In other words, in becoming man, Jesus voluntarily set aside His privileges of deity and restricted His divine prerogatives in order to fully experience life as we know it in a fallen and corrupt world. By coming among us in the flesh, Jesus showed us God's love in practical, tangible ways. As we shall see, it was the only way He could overcome sin and death for us to bring us back to God.

The second theme is *suffering*. Hebrews 2:10 says that God perfected Jesus, the author of our salvation, through suffering. Literally, the word *perfected* means *tested, qualified* and *approved*. Through his suffering, Jesus was qualified to be the author of our salvation. By identifying with our humanness and experiencing the full magnitude of human suffering and need, yet never failing, never refusing to obey His heavenly Father, and never reluctant to keep going, Jesus proved worthy to be our High Priest and Savior, the author of our salvation from sin, suffering and death. The term *author* means *the pioneer, the way-taker, the trailblazer, the point-man*.

Since you and I are flesh and blood, that is, human, God the Son had to become fully human, taking on flesh and blood and all our limitations. He came into the world as we did, nine months in the womb and through the birth canal of His mother. He got thirsty, hungry, and tired. He felt pain, physically and emotionally. He was susceptible to death. In fact, He died an awful death, crucified on a Roman cross. And this for a specific purpose: to render powerless the devil, who, for the time being, holds the power of death in that he gets us to sin and "the wages of sin is death" (Romans 6:23). Jesus, by going all the way through death, beat Satan at his own game and made it possible for us to overcome not only our own suffering and temptation, but death itself. Each Easter Sunday, we celebrate Christ's powerful resurrection from the dead. In His resurrection, Jesus broke the power of sin and death. He demonstrated that He was the winner. Nothing could stop Him and nothing could hold Him down. The same becomes true for those who receive Christ by faith, connect with His victorious life, and choose to follow Him. The Apostle Paul confirms this powerfully in 1 Corinthians 15:20-22: "But now Christ has been raised from the dead, the first fruits of those who have died. For since by a man came death, by a man also came the resurrection of the dead. For as in Adam all die, so also all in Christ will be made alive."

Jesus Understands because He Was Tested and Tempted in Every Way as We Are, Yet without Sin.

"For we do not have a high priest who cannot sympathize with our weaknesses, but One who has

been tempted in all things as we are, yet without sin." (Hebrews 4:15)

By suffering with us and for us, Christ was qualified to be our High Priest, the mediator between us and God the Father. The book of Hebrews describes Jesus as *merciful and compassionate,* because through His own suffering and trials, He can sympathize with all of ours and come to our aid. Think of some of the ways Jesus suffered that are similar to our own experiences: physical and emotional pain, rejection, misunderstanding, thought to be an illegitimate child by His Nazareth neighbors, let down and even abandoned by friends, and accused falsely. Yet, in spite of all of this, He is described as *faithful*—and this is most important—because, unlike us, Jesus never "blew it." Hebrews 4:15 says that Jesus was "tempted in all things as we are," yet with this important distinction, "without sin." No, he did not have people cutting him off in expressway traffic, nor the opportunity to file false returns with the IRS or fraudulent claims with an insurance company, nor did He have cable TV, movies, magazines or the Internet by which to access pornography. But all of these are mere modern mechanisms for age old temptations to sin the sins of anger, hatred, greed, dishonesty and lust. Yet, in one form or another, Jesus encountered all of these temptations. Most notably, he was tempted directly by Satan to avoid experiencing severe suffering in this life, to gain popularity by performing the stones-to-bread thing, to short-circuit death for our sins, and amass earthly wealth and power simply by changing allegiances from God the Father to himself. Jesus understands every level of temptation and suffering you know. Yet he never "caved" or gave in. He endured all the "stuff" of life without faltering, failing, sinning or refusing to obey. In a word, He was sinless. He followed His Father's plan and carried out His mission to seek and to save the lost by showing us God's love and sharing with us the Good News of salvation from sin and new life through Him; that in the face of fierce opposition and the pain of personal rejection. Therefore, as Hebrews 4:17 says, *in the things pertaining to God* He can be our representative and can take care of *our obligations* to God that we could not cover for ourselves. In fact, this same verse adds that Jesus made *propitiation* for people's sins. That is, by taking on our guilt and sins and absorbing God's wrath against them, He paid the penalty for our sin and deflected the judgment of God we deserved. Jesus understands.

Jesus Understands and Will Come to Our Aid as We Draw Near to His Throne of Grace

"For since He [Jesus] Himself was tempted in that which he has suffered, He is able to come to the aid of those who are tempted...Therefore, let us draw near with confidence to the throne of grace, so that we may receive mercy and find grace to help in time of need." (Hebrews 2:18; 4:16)

As we have seen already, Jesus Christ endured the severest temptations and testing life could deal out, particularly since He never gave in to them—experiencing temptation and suffering to the max. Time and time again, the temptation came to Him to choose a less costly way of fulfilling His heavenly calling, and to avert suffering and death. These temptations came not only from His adversary, the Devil, but from His own dear friends. Talk about peer pressure. But in every situation, Jesus' response was correct and consistent. Because Jesus succeeded in overcoming these temptations and trials, He can overcome anything at all. Consequently, when *we* experience trials, and when our doubts, personal pain or fears tempt us to lose faith and not follow what God has told us to do, we have only to call out to our great Savior, our pioneer, our way-taker, our champion, whom Hebrews 4:14 calls our Great High Priest.. We in the 21st century might find this a meaningless term, our eyes and minds glaze over as we hear it, and we might miss the point altogether. The term *Great High Priest* is rooted in Old Testament imagery. Understanding it in that context, we can appreciate fully what Christ has done and can do for us today. In Old Testament times, because God was not directly approachable by the people, the high priest represented the people by going to God for them and offering sacrifices to cover their sins. The main idea of the book of Hebrews is that the priesthood of Jesus is different and superior to that Old Testament priesthood. Not only is he the high priest who connects with us and God, but He is also the supreme sacrifice for our sin, a sacrifice only foreshadowed by those offered by previous high priests. Because of the absolute value and finality of

Jesus' sacrifice for our sins, He opened up the way to God, giving us *direct access to God* for everything we need. Therefore, because we have such a Great High Priest, we are extended the invitation in Hebrews 4:16, "Let us draw near with confidence to the throne of grace, so that we may receive mercy and find grace to help in time of need." The verb *draw near* is in a present continuous active tense—*keep on constantly drawing near.* How? With confidence and not fear. Where? To the throne, God's throne, the *throne of grace*—the place of open, free, undeserved favor. There you will find mercy and grace to help in anything you are experiencing because you have a sympathetic high priest, our great Savior, Jesus Christ. He is an immeasurable source of strength for us, because He has been there, He has taken the way, He has succeeded and He understands.

You may remember the nearly catastrophic lunar attempt for astronaut Jim Lovell and the rest of the Apollo 13 moon-shot crew. An explosion in the service module forced the crew to leave it and enter the lunar module. Conserving much-needed energy, they became subject to frigid temperatures as temperatures in outer space could be as low as nearly three hundred degrees below zero. Through a series of near disasters and makeshift temporary solutions, the crew was able to return to the service module, attempt to re-enter earth's atmosphere and return home. The obstacles were enormous, the odds against them seemingly insurmountable. The conditions of their environment restricted their ability to figure out all they needed to do. Things looked grim, three men about to be lost in space forever.

However, at the control center in Houston was another astronaut, Ken Mattingly, who had been scrubbed from the mission because he had been exposed to measles. Mattingly had the knowledge and experience to come to the aid of his fellow astronauts. But, as he climbed into the simulator, he said, make it cold and dark in here. Give me the same conditions those men up there are experiencing." After hours of painstaking work and struggle, with much going wrong, Mattingly finally resolved the problems and gave hope to the imperiled crew. Carefully, he gave instructions to his replacement in space. As the crew attempted to do what they needed to do, condensation, fatigue and foggy minds made it impossible even to read the instructions that they had written down. That is when Ken Mattingly said these memorable words from Houston: "Don't worry about it, Jack. I'll *talk* you through it." And he did exactly that. He knew what to do and how to do it because he had already done it under the same conditions they were in.

In your struggles, doubts, fears, or personal pain—pain inflicted by others and pain from your own choices—things that keep you from seeing and doing what God desires, Jesus is saying to you, "Don't worry, I will talk you through it." He knows what to do and how to do it because he has already done it under the same conditions you are in—and undoubtedly, in even far worse conditions. You don't need to fear; you don't need to be discouraged; you don't need to give up. If you are nearing the end of your rope, it's time to call upon the Lord. There is great victory in realizing the limits of your own ability — and the limitlessness of His. Christ is your source of wisdom, energy, encouragement and hope. He has been in your shoes and then some. No one understands like Jesus. You can trust Him with abandon. Hear Him say so tenderly, "Come unto me, all you who struggle and are heavily burdened and I will give you relief and rest." Bring your painful past to Jesus, whatever it might be. Let the pain of past failures, mistakes, and sins both small and monumental, as well as the pain inflicted on you by others, come to the surface. Meet these head on. Then, turn to the Savior who is there by your side. Tell Him all that troubles you. Ask for His forgiveness and cleansing. Ask him for a measure of His compassion and mercy as you recall someone who has hurt you, so that you can be merciful and forgiving toward them. Tell Him that you want to give your painful past to Him so that He can remove it as far as the East is from the West and heal your spirit and your memory. Today, we can say confidently that there is nothing that can defeat us or hold us back, no matter what we may face, no matter what life may bring. Jesus has blazed the trail. He is motioning right now to follow Him. Will you?

CHAPTER SEVEN:

ADOPTING HIS SERVANT-HEART

Ayoung Jewish mother was pushing along her identical twins in a stroller built for two, when she ran into a neighbor. "Oh, you had twins!" her neighbor exclaimed. "Yes," the young Jewish mother answers. "This is Jacob, the doctor and Reuben, the lawyer!" Now there's a good Jewish mother, picturing a very positive future for her sons.

In Matthew 20, the good Jewish mother who approaches Jesus was doing the same—pursuing a positive future—for her grown sons, James and John, who happened to be disciples of Jesus. She respectfully bows before Jesus to make a request— that her sons would be given preferential treatment and granted positions of privilege in Jesus' kingdom: "And Jesus said to her, 'What do you want?' She said to him, 'Say that these two sons of mine are to sit, one at your right hand and one at your left, in your kingdom'" (Matthew 20:20, 21). Sitting on Jesus' right and left hands suggests positions of highest authority and prestige in Christ's coming kingdom. It is important to notice the context of this conversation. "As Jesus was about to go up to Jerusalem, He took the twelve disciples aside and on the way He said to them, *'Behold, we are going up to Jerusalem; and the Son of Man will be delivered up to the chief priests and scribes, and they will condemn Him to death, and will deliver Him up to the Gentiles to mock and scourge and crucify Him, and on the third day He will be raised up"* (Matthew 20:17-19).

Jesus is heading toward Jerusalem and the final week of His passion on the *Via Dolorosa*, the Way of Suffering, leading to His awful crucifixion. He is preparing His disciples for these events by describing what was going to happen—His death sentence, His beatings, His terrible and tragic death. Then He adds that ray of hope, *"on the third day He will be raised again!"* Did these disciples even hear what He was saying? Were they so much like us, not "getting it" or even understanding what they were asking for? Or did they think that none of this would really happen, but rather, that Jesus would establish His kingdom instead? Whatever the case, these two, with the help of their mother, begin to vie for positions of importance in the kingdom. Imagine that. Yet we know that pride is an old enemy. It deceives us. It is never more odious than when it wears the cloak of religious service—people seeking position and recognition, but covering the self-seeking with spiritual jargon about God's will and serving Him. Yet, it is the selective service of religious pride that makes a pretense of humility, but doesn't understand what it really means to walk so closely to Christ that we really are on His left and right hands.

Jesus knew His own identity—Son of God and King of Glory—yet He responds to this presumptuous request most gently and humbly. He could have laughed at them, or put them in their place. But that was not His way. Rather, He quietly suggests directly to James and John that they do not know what they are asking.

Jesus Describes the Path to Greatness in His Kingdom

"Jesus answered and said, 'You do not know what you are asking for. Are you able to drink the cup that I am about to drink?' They said to Him, 'We are able'" (Matthew 20:22).

A prerequisite to reigning with Christ is to first suffer with Him. The road to Jesus' exaltation was deepest humiliation. Only the humblest of hearts would go the way He went. At this point, the disciples don't have a clue as to the extent Jesus would suffer. D. A. Carson points out that "in the spiritual arena, to ask for great usefulness and reward [including position] is often to ask for great suffering."[17] The *cup* of which Jesus spoke represents judgment and retribution at the hands of those opposed to Christ, resulting in Jesus' supreme suffering to secure our salvation. To begin with, the path to Christian greatness is not a glory road.

With foresight concerning their future identity with Him and what commitment to His service
means, Jesus indicates next that James and John
would indeed drink of that "cup" in a similar way.
*"He said to them, 'My cup you shall drink; but to sit
on My right and on My left, this is not Mine to give,
but it is for those for whom it has been prepared by My
Father"* (Matthew 20:23). Notice how Jesus makes
it clear that, although He is God the Son, yet in His
role as our servant-Savior, His is a derived authority.
Jesus knew His identity, yet served with humility. As
Christian creeds confirm, Jesus is "very God of very
God." He knew that. Yet even His role in the Trinity
is subservient to God the Father. Although He shares
the very essence of God, He voluntarily laid aside His
divine prerogatives as God to serve in humility. *"To
sit on my right and on my left is not mine to give…"*

The other disciples are listening in, as are we.
Upon hearing this exchange between James, John and
Jesus, they become indignant and apparently begin to
squabble over issues of importance, position and leadership. The way Jesus responds to this gives us the
sense that their indignation and anger is not so much
from their concern for justice or equity, but for their
own self-interests and pride. The entire situation presents Jesus with a teaching moment for them and for
us. *"But Jesus called them to Himself, and said, 'You
know that the rulers of the Gentiles lord it over them,
and their great men exercise authority over them. It
is not so among you, but whoever wishes to become
great among you shall be your servant, and whoever
wishes to be first among you shall be your slave…"*

(Matthew 20:25-27). In a sentence Jesus reverses all human ideas of greatness and rank. What is true in the world in which you live, Jesus says, where authority and position mean exercising lordship over someone else, will *not* be true for my followers. The structures of a culture, be they ever so necessary in government, cannot be brought over into the kingdom of God or the Church. Rather, Jesus again makes it absolutely clear: greatness among Jesus' people is based on service and servanthood. He knew what Scripture says, that God resists the proud, but gives grace to the humble. It is this attitude of genuine humility in stark contrast to the me-first disposition of the culture that made Jesus so attractive and compelling. It is undoubtedly why self-giving individuals like Sister Maria Teresa are so highly regarded and revered in the Christian community and in the world. Jesus makes the way clear. "Anyone who wishes to be great among you shall be your servant." The word *servant* means, *one who humbly helps*. Jesus strengthens the intention of His meaning by using a different and stronger word in verse 27: *"Whoever wishes to be first among you shall be your slave."*

It has been said well, "The person who is too big for the small job is too small for a big one." Many Christians today balk at the idea of being in a subservient role inside or outside the church and Christ's kingdom. We may wonder, as Ruth Harms Calkin ruminates in the poem, "I Wonder":

You know, Lord, how I serve You
With great emotional fervor
In the limelight.
You know how eagerly I speak for You
At a women's club.
You know how I effervesce when I promote
A fellowship group.
You know my genuine enthusiasm
At a Bible study
But how would I react, I wonder
If you pointed to a basin of water
And asked me to wash the calloused feet
Of a bent and wrinkled old woman
Day after day
Month after month
In a room where nobody saw
And nobody knew.

The idea of doing menial tasks for the benefit of someone else, or extending oneself to the lowly and unlovely is not at all attractive. It is easier to withhold ourselves from the needy or those who we find socially unacceptable. Somehow we may even feel that because we are Christians, we are better than those who are still practicing the kinds of sins that repulse us. Nevertheless, humble servanthood toward all others, says Jesus, is prerequisite to priority in Christ's kingdom.

Jesus' ethics of leadership and influence in the Christian community are revolutionary to say the least. That is why when those in leadership in the Christian community, at home, in the church, on the job, or in their community, become bossy, bullying, tyrannical or even despotic, they are not exercising Biblical authority, but abusing it. It is why, when Christians withhold themselves from the poor, the downtrodden and the broken, when we avoid the unlovely and cling tenaciously to the comfort and security of our in-church activities and private lives, that we miss the path to greatness in Christ's kingdom, find ourselves walking where Jesus is not walking, and wonder what is wrong. It is why so often, Christians individually and church congregations collectively fail to connect with non-Christian people around them and do not make an impact on their world for Christ. Look at where Jesus walked. Look at the way Jesus lived.

Jesus Leads Us in the Way of Humility and Humble Service by His Own Example

"The Son of Man did not come to be served, but to serve, and to give His life a ransom for many" (Matthew 20:28).

Let me repeat: Jesus knew His identity, yet served with humility. What Jesus taught, He demonstrated in His life—mercy, forgiveness and unselfish concern for others. He said that a person who wished to follow Him must deny himself, take up his cross daily, and follow Him. He presents Himself as the supreme example of godly service and leadership. Although He is the Lord, He states clearly in this verse that He "came not to be served, but to serve and to give Himself...." I had to ask myself, "Does that describe me? Don't I prefer to be comfortable? Don't I relish the privacy of my backyard that keeps me secluded from my neighbors? Aren't I frustrated by the phone call that intrudes into my leisure and requires a response that will inconvenience me?" Yet, far beyond mere inconvenience, Jesus laid down His life for us as a "ransom," –a price paid to set slaves free. We are those slaves. Because of His loving, self-giving servanthood, Jesus was very attractive, not to the proud and self-righteous, but to the downcast sinners who knew they needed a Savior but were not finding much care and compassion from the religious community. Those are the people who will respond to us and to our message today when we, knowing our identity as children of the King and citizens of His kingdom, come to them with compassion and kindness, and serve them with humility. Only then will we have the privilege of walking where Jesus walks.

The Apostle Paul understood where Jesus is leading us when he wrote in 2 Corinthians 5:14, 15 that Christ died for all *"so that they who live might no longer live for themselves...."* He follows this in 2 Corinthians 8:9 with one of the most powerful descriptions of the idea that Jesus knew His identity, yet served with humility: *"For you know the Grace of our Lord Jesus Christ, that though He was rich, yet for your sake He became poor, that you through His poverty might become rich."*

Jesus leads us in the way of humility and humble service by His own example. Although He was rich and prominent as the Lord of glory, He chose poverty and humility. Though a King, He became a servant.

Entitled to rule, He identified with the lowly, coming to give and even to die. Why? For you and me—for our sakes; for our well-being. He meets us at the point of our greatest need and meets that need. What did it take for Jesus to come to us this way? Let me paraphrase how the great British preacher of the past, Charles Spurgeon put it when teaching on this verse:

The Lord Jesus Christ, then was rich. We all believe that. Oh, how surprised the angels were, when they were first informed that Jesus Christ, the Prince of Light and Majesty, intended to clothe himself in clay and become a human baby and live and die. What? Was it true that He whose crown was studded with the stars of heaven would lay that crown aside? What? Was it certain that He around whose shoulders was cast the royal purple of the universe, would become a man dressed in peasant's garments? Could it be true that He who was everlasting and immortal would one day be nailed to a cross? Look! He who created all things has now become so weak that a woman must carry him. She carries him to Egypt to preserve his life. Now see him who made the worlds handling the hammer and the nails, assisting his father in the trade of a carpenter. Look at him, Christian. Follow him through his entire journey. Go with him in the wilderness of temptation. See him fasting there and hungering with wild beasts all around. Follow him along his wearying way, as the Man of Sorrows acquainted with grief. He is the swear word of the scorner; the brunt of false accusations and mean-spirited jokes. Yet, see him as a servant, touching the sick, the lame, the poor and the down-trodden. He, the prince of peace, is mingling with the worst of sinners. He who had once been served by angels, becomes the servant of servants. Taking a towel and a basin of water, he washes the dirty feet of sinful men. He who was once honored with the hallelujahs of the heavens, is now spit upon and despised. Oh, for the words to picture the humiliation of Christ! What miles of distance between him who sat on the throne of heaven and him who now dies upon the cross! Who can tell the mighty chasm between the heights of his glory and the cross of deepest agony? Follow Him, Christian. Follow him along his path of suffering until at last you meet him among the olives of Gethsemane; see him sweating great drops of blood! Follow him to the pavement of Gabbatha; see him pouring out rivers of gore beneath the cruel whips of Roman soldiers! With weeping eyes, follow him to the cross of Calvary. See him nailed there! Mark his poverty, so poor that they have stripped him naked from head to foot and exposed him to the face of the sun. So poor, that when he asks them for water, they give him vinegar to drink. So poor that his unpillowed head is crowned with thorns in death. Oh, Son of Man, I do not know which to admire most—your height of glory, or your depths of misery for my sake. Oh, Man, slain for us; shall we not exalt you, God over all, blessed forever? Shall we not give you our loudest song, our very best love and our humblest service? "He was rich, yet for your sakes he became poor."[18]

In a poignant moment on the eve of His death, Jesus dramatized the humble servant attitude *he* wants us to adopt, by giving us a memorable object lesson. *"Jesus...rose from supper and laid aside his garments; and taking a towel, girded Himself with it. Then He poured water into the basin and began to wash the disciples' feet, and to wipe them with the towel with which He was girded"* (John 13:3-5).

It was during the evening before His horrible death that Jesus gathered His followers together to share the Passover meal with them and to pour out to them the ardor of His heart, like a passionate parent preparing his teen age sons for the future, passing on to them, and now to us, the dreams He has for His people—His Church. During this supper, He again calls us to adopt His servant heart with uncommon love for one another and by serving one another.

In the course of the evening, as Jesus broke the bread and blessed the cup, infusing these elements of the Jewish Passover meal with new, eternal significance, Luke's account of the Last Supper tells us that a dispute broke out among Jesus' disciples as to which one of them should be considered the greatest. Remember that these were not average, fair-weather Christians. They were devoted followers who had left jobs and creature comforts to follow Christ. Yet, even they were plagued by that perpetual nemesis, our self-imposed enemy, Pride. Pride in the form of selfish ambition was turning the heads of these devoted followers at the very moment when God the Son was about to lay down His life for them and us. Isn't it amazing that after all the time the disciples had spent with Jesus and observed His servant-heart, He still had to confront their attitudes of superiority and ambition? And what would He say to us when we seek our own interests ahead of His and regard ourselves as more important than those around us? Jesus was constantly dealing with the ego issues of His first followers. He continues to do so with Christians today.

The Bible tells us that Jesus got up from the table, took three common objects, a pitcher of water, a bowl and a towel, got down on His hands and knees and began washing their feet. Those bickering followers must have been stunned to silence. Here, in a simple, wordless act of self-effacing service, Jesus demonstrates the loving servanthood to which He is calling us all — to love one another by serving one another. Again, it is Luke who tells us that Jesus then repeats a lesson He had already taught them before saying,

"The rulers of the Gentiles lord it over them...but it will not be so with you. Rather, let him who is the greatest among you become as the youngest, and the leader as the servant. For who is greater, the one who reclines at the table or the one who serves? Is it not the one who reclines at the table? But I am among you as one who serves" (Luke 22:25-27).
"And so when Jesus had washed their feet...He said to them, 'Do you know what I have done to you? You call Me Teacher and Lord; and you are right; for so I am. If I then, the Lord and the Teacher, washed your feet, you also ought to wash one another's feet. For I gave you an example that you also should do as I

did to you...A slave is not greater than his master;
neither one who is sent greater than the one who sent
him. If you know these things, blessed are you if you
do them'" (John 13:12-17).

Jesus says to them in so many words, "Do you get it? If I, your Lord and Master would do this, could you possibly be exempt? Not a chance!" As Oswald Chambers observes, "Our Lord did not say, 'I have had a most successful time here on earth; I've addressed thousands of people and have been the means of their salvation; now go and do the same.' He said, 'If I then your Lord and Master have washed your feet, you also ought to wash one another's feet.'"[19]

I recall re-enacting this foot-washing scene during a communion service. I asked for a volunteer from the congregation. A young man came to the front of the sanctuary, sat down on a chair I had provided, and removed his shoes and socks. As I got down on my knees and began to wash his feet, I looked up at his face. Tears were streaming down. Later he told me, "It took me by surprise, seeing you and imagining my Lord...I couldn't contain my emotions." Until that moment, he knew only the "disconnect" that is familiar to us all, being acquainted with the Bible story and lesson, intellectually cognitive of its calling on our lives, but out of touch with the reality of the experience, the implications of that reality, and the impact of the experience. There is power in humble self-giving servanthood.

Again, Oswald Chambers remarks, "Sometimes Christians are even willing to wash the heathen's feet in another land, or feet in the slums. But fancy washing the feet in relationships more immediate and personal and perhaps more difficult—a husband's feet, or a wife's; the feet of a difficult member in the church."[20] I have to agree. Most often, humbling ourselves in those relationships is much more difficult. However, in calling us to His kind of servant love, Jesus topples four large gods in our lives—*I, me, mine and myself*—because, at the root of human problems is selfishness—especially in the area of our relationships with God and others. That is why Jesus, when calling us into His life, tells us that we must deny ourselves. However, the very thing that needs to be cured in us is the very thing that gets in the way of the cure. The irony is that while servanthood is the antidote to selfishness, selfishness is the obstacle to servanthood.

Charles Swindoll writes in his book *Improving Your Serve,* "Jesus longs for us to be different; not a getter, but a giver; not one who holds a grudge, but a forgiver; not one who keeps score, but a forgetter; not a superstar, but a servant."[21]

When the early followers of Jesus saw the value and necessity of this posture of humble, loving servanthood in the Church, they wrote to us in their own words, as directed by the Spirit of God, a wealth of instruction on the subject throughout the New Testament. Here is a sampling of key phrases: *Have affection for one another; in honor, give preference to one another; be of the same mind with one another; don't judge one another; follow after peace with one another; build up one another, receive one another, accept one another, greet one another with a holy kiss; care for one another, bear with one another; bear up one another; comfort one another, pray for one another, serve one another; love one another.* Implementing these attitudes and actions of Christian humility will cultivate in us the art of unselfish living. It is to this that Christ calls us.

Of course, washing the disciples' feet was merely a one-act dramatization of our Lord's entire life of self-giving love and service. He is calling us to something He has modeled completely. *"Have this attitude in you which was also in Christ Jesus, who, although He existed in the form of God, did not regard equality with God a thing to be grasped, but emptied Himself, taking the form of a bond-servant, and being made in the likeness of men. And being found in appearance as a man, He humbled Himself by becoming obedient to the point of death, even death on a cross"* (Philippians 2:5-8).

Do we understand the secret to such humble serving? Jesus relinquished His personal rights and divine prerogatives. He let go. Jesus humbled Himself as a servant. Jesus obeyed His heavenly Father at the greatest personal cost possible—unto death, even death on the cross! Why? For you and for me. Does our familiarity with this idea distance us from its implications? The Apostle Peter writes, *"For you have been called for this purpose, since Christ also suffered for you, leaving you an example for you to follow in His steps"* (1 Peter 2:21). For Jesus, the way of servanthood was the way of the cross. That is why, for us to answer His call to loving servanthood, we must die to self and say from our hearts,

"For me, to live *is* Christ, and to die is gain!" The best test is for each of us to ask ourselves if we are willing to humble ourselves and lovingly serve today the person toward whom we would find it most difficult. It might be your spouse, someone in the church, a family member, a neighbor, a classmate or someone at work. We may struggle just like those first devoted followers of Jesus did. Nevertheless, getting into Jesus' life includes adopting His servant heart.

The loving, humble servanthood to which Jesus calls us serves a powerful purpose. Jesus said, *"By this everybody will know that you are my disciples."* People need to see spiritual reality in the lives of Jesus' followers. Jesus says they will when they see Christians who love and serve each other and their neighbors like this.

Toward the end of 2 Corinthians the Apostle Paul writes, *"I will most gladly spend and be expended for your souls."* And we reply, "Okay! How far will you go? What sacrifices are you willing to make?" Here is Paul's response in expanded terms to capture the Greek phrases he uses: "I am overjoyed to spend everything I have and everything I am until I am completely spent, depleted, exhausted and have nothing left—for your sakes." When we can say that to people around us who need our love, our compassion, and our Savior, then we will shine with the attractiveness of our Lord, who knew His real identity, yet served with humility, giving His all for our sakes.

Do you know who you are? In Christ you are child of royalty, a person of prestige, an heir of the King of kings. That is a place of high honor and supreme social status in God's economy. If you know your identity, you won't have to assert it. Rather, you will want to be like your Master—servant of all.

CHAPTER EIGHT:

EMBRACING HIS MISSION

At the onset of the Civil War, one of Abraham Lincoln's aides said to the sixteenth President, "I hope God is on our side." To which Lincoln replied, "To the contrary, sir, I hope we are on His." That difference in perspectives is similar to where we began in this book: the premise that Christ does not ask us to invite Him into our lives to help us fulfill our dreams. Rather, He calls us to deny ourselves and get into His life, following Him (Mark 8: 34, 35). It is in getting into His life that He, in turn, gets into ours and transforms us into His likeness.

Responding to God's enormous love for us so eloquently displayed on the cross of Christ where He laid down His life for us, we respond in faith, turn from our sins, take up our crosses of self-denial and ego death, and are immersed into the life of Jesus to follow Him. In doing so, we become part of the people of God who are, in some sense, His continuing incarnation—the life of God being lived out in the lives of Christians.

Now I propose that, trusting Jesus Christ with abandon because we abide in His love for us, we will embrace and continue Christ's mission. "Mission Control" is the church to which we belong whose mission is to *"make disciples [devoted followers of Christ] of all nations..."* (Matthew 28:19). We are the mission operatives. Our code word is *compassion*. Your mission, should you accept it, is outlined by Jesus Himself in Luke 4, and described even further in Matthew 25 and 28.

"Jesus returned to Galilee in the power of the Spirit; and news about Him spread through all the surrounding district. And He began teaching in their synagogues and was praised by all. And he came to Nazareth, where He had been brought up; and as was His custom, He entered the synagogue on the Sabbath, and stood up to read. The book of the prophet Isaiah was handed to Him. He opened the book and found the place where it was written. 'The Spirit of the Lord is upon Me, because He anointed Me to preach the Good News to the poor. He has sent Me to proclaim release to the captives, and recovery of sight to the blind, to set free those who are downtrodden, and to proclaim the year of the Lord's favor.' And He said to them, 'Today this Scripture has been fulfilled in your hearing'" (Luke 4:14-21).

When he was only twelve, Jesus revealed to His parents the driving impulse, the sense of urgency that beat within his youthful heart: "I must be about my Father's business" (Luke 2:49 KJV). Then, at the outset of His ministry, and again at the close, Jesus delineated His mission and revealed the passion of His heart and the purpose of His coming. He did this in the synagogue of His hometown, Nazareth, where He was handed the scroll of the book of Isaiah. Jesus read a portion that speaks of the coming Messiah and describes Messiah's ministry. As Jesus read these words from Isaiah 61, his listeners would have understood the context of this eloquent prophetic passage—the Year of Jubilee, "the year of the Lord's favor." Announced on the Day of Atonement, the year of Jubilee was a time when debts were forgiven, property was restored, and slaves were redeemed and released. The words of Isaiah describe a man who is anointed by the Spirit of God specifically for the honor of proclaiming the good news of forgiveness, freedom and favor. The speaker in the passage is the coming Servant of the Lord who will bring these glad tidings to oppressed people during tough times with the promise, "It will be alright! The Lord's favor is coming, because the Lord's Messiah is coming! He will lift you up, give you sight, heal you and set you free." Those benefiting from his coming are described as poor, broken-hearted, captives and prisoners. Now Jesus identifies Himself as this one who was anointed by God's Spirit to bring these promised results. By connecting Himself to this prophecy, Jesus is saying, "The time has come. I am here. It's Jubilee!" Is it any wonder that those who responded positively to Jesus were not the religious and self-righteous, but the down and outers who had no where to go but up? They knew they were blind, down-trodden and enslaved. Because of that, they would embrace Jesus by faith and be set free.

It is important that we understand what Jesus says here because this is the mission into which He is leading us as we get into Jesus' life. This is the passion He wants to stir up in our hearts as we respond to His love and trust Him with abandon. We will know that we have gotten into Jesus' life and are actually embracing His mission when we are engaged in the five areas of compassionate service identified by Jesus before His home crowd. As you read on, God may touch your heart and give it a tug as you see Christ's mission, feel His passion, and realize that He has passed on the baton of this calling to us Christians. As we hear what Jesus came to do, our own imaginations will be captured. Be prepared to write down what God might be saying to you personally. You will find yourself thinking of ways that some of these things should be done here and now, and how you might participate in them or actually make them happen, because you are following Christ. As we hear from Jesus right now, ask yourself, "How am I now participating, or how can I be engaged in each of these actions?" The first action Jesus describes in His mission and calls us to continue is

Share the Good News with the Poor

"He has appointed Me to preach the Good News to the poor." The "good news" is that we can be pardoned by God and completely forgiven of all our

sins. Consequently, each of us can be reconciled to or made right with God and enjoy a relationship with Him as our loving heavenly Father. This is because Jesus, the Son of God, offered up on the cross His sinless life of perfect obedience to God the Father in payment for the guilt of our sin against God. While on earth, Jesus reached out to the physically and materially poor, meeting them at their point of immediate need — food, health, physical impairment — so that He could touch a much deeper need, their spiritual poverty before God. He didn't exclude the wealthy. He simply knew that the more people have, the slower they seem to respond to the good news (Luke 18:24-27). Their wealth distracts them from God and gives them a sense of self-sufficiency. Yet, the real meaning here is for us to share the Good News with those who are poor *in spirit*, who recognize their spiritual bankruptcy before God, and who need the insurmountable debt of their sin fully paid by the One who in love came to rescue them. All around us there are spiritually poverty-stricken people who need to know that regardless of what they have or do not have materially, they are in want of God's pardon, cleansing and refurbishing. The hunger they feel inside will be satisfied by nothing else. We have good news for them. When we energetically, creatively, and passionately tell them the good news of life in Christ, we embrace and continue the mission that Jesus began and passed on to us. Share the good news with the spiritually impoverished. The next action Jesus describes in His mission and calls us to continue is

Tell the Enslaved that They Can Be Free

"He has sent Me to proclaim release to the captives." To be pardoned and set free is for prisoners. The most obvious application of this action would be ministry to those in our jails. We can surmise that Jesus had that specific ministry in his mind and heart as He read these words. Hebrews 13:2 says, *"Remember the prisoners as though you were in prison with them."* Perhaps God would nudge you today toward jail ministry. However, not all prisoners are in jails. Many people are enslaved to all kinds of things, bound by attitudes that hold them captive, harmful habits that clutch them in a viselike grip. There are people who are locked into patterns of poisonous hate or bitter resentments, possessive greed and selfish ambition. Others are caught in the bondage of life-controlling problems or addictions to pornography, alcohol, gambling and the like. Still others are trying to free themselves from the guilt and shame of past sins. Jesus has something to say to each of these. He can set them free! The power by which He broke the bands of death and got up out of the grave, is the power He brings to the life of the soul-tortured person who turns to Him, trusts in Him, and in faith, asks Jesus Christ to pardon him and set him free. Jesus can turn the key in any prison door and release the captives. Jesus' work is the work of those who are His, who have gotten into His life. We embrace and continue His mission when we open ourselves up to people in bondage of any kind to tell them that the love and power and pardon of Christ can set them free. Tell the enslaved that they can be

free indeed! A third action that Jesus describes in His mission and calls us to continue is

Give Sight to Those Who Cannot See

"He sent Me to proclaim...recovery of sight to the blind." Jesus actually did restore sight to people who were literally blind. Occasionally, He gives us the privilege of participating in the physical healing of sick or impaired people. But one thing Jesus made clear was that His ministry to people's physical needs was simply a compassionate demonstration of His ability to meet their much deeper spiritual needs. Jesus fed 5,000 with five loaves and two fish. (I recently heard of a little boy who said that was nothing. His mother did that every year with Thanksgiving leftovers!) Jesus did the physical miracle, and then said, "I am the bread of life. If you partake of Me, you'll never hunger again." He healed the blind person and then said, "I am the light of the world," "I am the way, the truth and the life." Jesus is able to give insight and understanding of what is true and real to those who are spiritually blind and lack the understanding of what life is really all about. Do you know people like that—people who are groping, looking for answers in all the wrong places? When you see someone who is physically blind, you want to go over to assist him. Those who are spiritually blind need someone to come alongside them and show them the light of God's truth; someone who can make sense out of life, because God has already given that insight to him. In John 8:12 Jesus says, "If

anyone follows me, he shall not walk in darkness, but shall have the light of life." As we get into His life and embrace His mission, we will befriend non-Christians and the irreligious in our neighborhoods, workplaces and schools in order to shine the light of God's truth into their lives by our words and by our compassionate actions and examples. We will look for creative ways to show them tangibly the nature of God's unconditional love by surprising them with our unexpected acts of kindness and love and by treating them the way we ourselves would love to be treated. By these we will show them the reality of our lives in Christ and warm their hearts to the good news we have to share with them concerning the salvation Christ gives. Embracing Christ's mission means giving sight and insight to those who cannot see. Still another action that Jesus describes in His mission and calls us to continue is

Deliver Those Who Are Oppressed and Down and Out

"To set free those who are downtrodden." There is no question that Jesus had in mind those in our world who are suffering unjustly and need peace, encouragement, hope and release from their oppressors. That is why Christians engage in world relief, peace and justice issues, and social reform. But what Jesus does goes even deeper. In the sense the word is used here, to be *oppressed* carries a demonic element and is often experienced as being weighed down in your spirit, dejected, depressed and despairing. A

sense of hopelessness and worthlessness may accompany these. Sometimes people give Satan a toehold in their lives through unresolved conflict, anger turned inward, bitterness toward another person, or unconfessed sin (cf. Ephesians 4:26,27). In his book titled *Body Life,* author Ray Stedman tells of such a person.[22] Stedman relates how this man was delivered, describing him as one who for over a year he had been terribly affected by an attitude of hate toward a man who had done him a great injustice. His bitterness toward the man left him sleepless, troubling him with constant depression and despair, plaguing him with dark thoughts of murder. It was breaking him up, destroying his family and threatening his own life. With the truth of the Scripture about his unforgiving spirit, Pastor Stedman gently explained to him that he was poisoning his own life by his hatred and that there could be no release till he was able to forgive the man who had offended him. He agreed to ask God for the grace to do so—and they prayed together. As they prayed, the man was healed and his was burden lifted. The oppressed was set free. His whole attitude visibly changed as hate drained out of that man's heart and the love of Jesus Christ come flooding in. The man was delivered from his oppression by the power of Christ through the efforts of a person who had gotten into Jesus' life and embraced His mission to deliver those who are oppressed and down and out. The last important action that Jesus describes in His mission and calls us to continue is

Announce the Time of God's Grace— His Favor

"To proclaim the favorable year of the Lord." Jesus was reading Isaiah 61 from the scroll that had been handed to Him. If you were to look at that chapter yourself, you would discover that the passage says, "To proclaim the favorable year of the Lord *and* the day of the vengeance of our God." First, grace and favor, then judgment. But Jesus stops short of the judgment and vengeance of God against our sins, because His mission the first time He came to this earth was to announce the grace of God toward us sinners. In John 3:17 we read: "God did not send His Son into the world to condemn the world, but that the world might be saved through Him. Through Christ's self-sacrifice on the cross, people could be forgiven, cleansed on the inside, made right with God and given eternal life—all things we do not deserve but are given freely because of God's favor toward us, His grace. Jesus' message is clear, "He who believes in Me (that is, trusts me with abandon by throwing himself on me in faith) is not condemned." The Apostle Paul reiterates that promise when in Romans 8:1 his pen soars with the good news, "Therefore, there is now no condemnation for those who are *in Christ Jesus.*" When Jesus comes again, it will be to gather to Himself those who have trusted in Him and have gotten into His life, and to judge the rest of world. But between His first coming and His Second Coming is the era of God's grace, the age in which we now live. God is giving everyone of us a chance to turn from his or her own ways to His way; from

self-centeredness to Christ-centeredness, from darkness to light, from death to life. And He has passed on to us the mission of announcing this good news to as many people as possible. People need to know what Scripture states plainly, *"Today* is the day of salvation," a time of God's kindness, patience, mercy and grace (2 Corinthians 6:2). Christ announced this good news to everyone He saw. Getting into His life, and trusting Him with abandon, we will do the same. It is a significant part of the mission we now embrace.

Most people who are not followers of Christ know deep within themselves that they are not acceptable to a Holy God. Thousands upon thousands of people are gripped with the cold fear of dying and plunging into an unknown eternity. They wonder about the significance of this life and what awaits them after death. Often, they joke about it; but the inevitability nags them. They fear tomorrow. They fear death. They fear the judgment of God. People need to know, not that they are on the outs with God, but that this is the period of God's loving favor. For the time being, God has suspended judgment and is extending mercy. They need to know that while God hates their sin, He loves them so much that He has moved heaven and earth to do something about the consequences of that sin. *"God demonstrated His love toward us in that while we were yet sinners, Christ died for us"* (Romans 5:8). This ministry of Christ's compassionate grace is the mission we embrace and continue when people see evidence of God's love and grace in our lives. They see us uncommonly loving, patient, merciful and forgiving toward one another and very open and non-judgmental toward them. As we embrace His mission of compassion, we become the showcases of God's grace and love. An increasingly angry, violent, bitter and unforgiving world comes to understand God's grace as they see it and feel it from us. Then, they will listen as they hear from us how, through Christ, the same thing can be true for them because this is the time of God's grace. We have a mission to embrace today.

Jesus could say in Luke 4:21, *"Today this Scripture is fulfilled in your hearing,"* because *He* was the fulfillment of Isaiah's prophecy describing the mission and passion of the Messiah. That is because the very first thing He read from Isaiah was true of Him (v. 18): *"The Spirit of the Lord is upon Me."* Jesus did not carry out this mission of compassion by His own self-engendered initiative. It was by the power of the Holy Spirit of God upon Him and within Him that Jesus accomplished His mission. When He passed the baton of compassionate ministry to us, He said in Acts 1:8, *"You shall receive power after the Holy Spirit has come upon you, and you shall* (in so many words) *continue what I have begun."* We have been loved by Christ our self-giving servant. His trademark is compassion. He simply asks us to love others, to genuinely care about their well-being and eternal destiny, even at our own expense and inconvenience, in the same way that He has loved us. Responding to His enormous love for us, we trust Him with abandon. Trusting Him with abandon, we deny ourselves and get into His life. Getting into His life, He gets into ours and we embrace His mission of compassion to the desperately needy people all around us. It is the reflexive response of the person who has completely aligned himself with Christ's life and mission. It is then that we experience the joy of serving Christ in the power of the Holy Spirit, to the praise of His glory.

The question is, how will we respond? It is time for a mission operatives' report: Christian, how have you done so far in embracing Christ's mission of compassion and announcing good news? What has Christ prompted within your heart as you have read this chapter? But be careful here. Far too often we respond to a call to embrace Christ's mission on an "ought to" basis, with fear or guilt as the principle motivators. Fear tells us, "You better do this!" Guilt tells us, "You never do this!" There is a deeper, more profound and far more effective motivation: being moved by the incomparable, incomprehensible love of Christ for us. The Apostle Paul put it this way in 2 Corinthians 5, when describing why he and his cohorts had embraced the compassionate mission of Christ wholeheartedly: *"The love of Christ compels us. After all, He died for us so that we who live should no longer live for ourselves but for Him who died and rose again on our behalf."*

Do you see it? Fear and guilt foster grudging duty. The love of Christ produces compassionate service. In his excellent book *Your God is Too Safe,* Mark Buchanan asserts, "I contend this: scratch the most vigorous, authentic Christian you know, and he or she will bleed love—love for God, love for others, and a deep conviction about God's love for him or her. And the opposite: scratch the sourest, most sedentary Christian you know, and he or she will bleed guilt."[23] Buchanan observes that this was a distinguishing difference between Jesus and the Pharisees that went beyond the Pharisees' focus on the externals and Jesus' concern for the issues of the heart. The Pharisees practiced an ethic of avoidance, Jesus, an ethic of involvement. They asked, "How can I keep from annoying or aggravating God?" Jesus asked, "How can I glorify God?" They questioned, "How can I keep from being contaminated by the riff-raff of the world?" Jesus asked, "How can I reach the riff-raff and make them clean?" The Pharisees asked, "How can I steer clear of sinners and maintain the religious status quo?" Jesus asked, "where do I need to go, what do I need to do to make an eternal difference in the lives of lost and hurting people?" The Pharisees were concerned about avoiding sinning or the appearances of sin. Jesus was concerned about rescuing the perishing.

In a graphic manner found in Matthew 25: 31-40, Jesus distinguishes the sheep from the goats, the godly from the ungodly: *"When the Son of Man comes in His glory, and all the angels with Him, then He will sit on His glorious throne. And all the nations will be gathered before him; and He will separate them from one another, as the shepherd separates the sheep from the goats; and He will put the sheep on His right, and the goats on the left. Then the King will say to those on His right, 'Come, you who are blessed of My Father, inherit the kingdom prepared for you from the foundation of the world. For I was hungry, and you gave Me something to eat; I was thirsty, and you gave Me drink; I was a stranger, and you invited Me in; naked, and you clothed Me. I was sick and you visited Me; I was in prison, and you came to Me.' Then the righteous will answer Him saying, 'Lord, when did we see you hungry and feed You, or thirsty, and give you drink? When did we see You a stranger and invite You in, or naked and clothe you? And when did we see You sick, or in prison, and come to you?' And the king will answer and say to them, 'Truly I say to you, to the extent that you did it to one of these brothers of Mine, even the least of them, you did it to Me.'"* Notice that in that day when we stand in the literal presence of Jesus, He doesn't commend people for annual income, business successes, athletic accomplishments or the like. Rather, he praises the initiatives that characterized his own mission—ministering to the poor, the hurting, the oppressed and downtrodden. Christ's compassionate love to others will be real and measurable in our lives, not simply theoretical, when we get into His life and embrace His mission.

Helmut Thielicke observes this about Christ. "He came into the world through its most hidden door. He was born a poor child in a little hole-and-corner town on the edge of the world. He comforted the weeping, blessed the children, and laid his hand upon the despairing. But these poor, sick, miserable people are not to be found on the avenue of triumph where kings come marching in. They shuffle and crouch in the dark and hidden corners, they live in the attics and barracks of the poor, and sometimes, of course, in the loneliness of an executive's office."[24] Christ's presence made a difference wherever He went in this broken and heart-breaking world with all its seediness and neediness. Does your presence make that difference too? He tells us that He came to seek and to save the lost. Motivated by His love, trusting Him with abandon, getting into His life so that He can get into ours, we will make a difference.

In his Gospel, Mark writes this: *"And Jesus went up to the mountain and called those whom He Himself wanted, and they came to Him. And He appointed them that they might be with Him, and that He might send them out…"* (Mark 3:13, 14). First, Jesus' followers were *with Him*, spending time in His presence. Then He sent them out. First Christ says to us, "Come unto Me." Then He says, "Go out for Me." Jesus could not have been clearer when He said, *"As you are going into all the world, announce the good news and make disciples."* (Matthew 28:19), and *"As the Father has sent Me, so send I you"* (John 20:21). As we spend time with Him, marinating in His love, He rubs off on us and gets into the very fiber of who we are. Then we go out and rub Him off on others, His cleanness and love spilling out of us with compassion. We tell people about His favor. We share with them the Good News. The blind see. The oppressed are delivered. The captives are set free!

PRAYER: *Lord Christ, may your love overwhelm us so that we trust you with abandon, get into your life, and embrace your mission of compassion, showing your love and announcing the good news of your* *favor toward us sinners to everyone we see. May we hear with clarity your words, "As the Father has sent Me, so send I you." Amen.*

CHAPTER NINE:

PARTICIPATING IN HIS STRATEGY— MAKE DISCIPLES

Jim and Steve are brothers just two years apart, Jim being the older. They were raised in a church-going family and participated in the church's youth program. Within the context of that program, each heard the Gospel of Jesus Christ and decided to follow Jesus. Now in their early forties, there is a marked difference in their spiritual lives. Jim still attends church and occasionally gets involved in some of the church's programs and ministries. But outside of church it is difficult to distinguish him from his business partner who describes himself as agnostic. Jim's focus is on building a secure financial life and retiring early in order to enjoy several recreational interests he has—golfing, boating, and travel. Steve's faith, on the other hand, is unmistakable. A non-negotiable part of his daily schedule is time spent in prayer, in Bible study and in meditation, reflecting on God's truth that he has mined from that study. He loves to talk to others about his relationship to Jesus Christ and is eager to show the love of Christ to others in practical, self-giving ways. While he has provided adequately for his family, he has adopted as his motto for the future, "Don't retire, retool" with a view toward being able to use the added discretionary time of his retirement years to invest his vocational skills in areas of Christian ministry without compensation. What do you suppose made the difference in the spiritual pilgrimages of these brothers? Simply this: along with a couple of other young men, Steve was discipled by a spiritually mature fellow Christian for several years. Jim was not. Steve followed the example set for him by becoming a "discipler" himself. Jim didn't even consider it. Unfortunately, disciple-making was not characteristic of the church they attended. With which of these two brothers can you most identify?

Jesus summed up the mission to which He has called His followers with these succinct marching orders, "Make disciples!" He couched this call in the context of His ascending into heaven and sending the Holy Spirit to live within those who believe in and follow Him, so that we could carry on with divine power the kingdom ministry He began (Matthew 28:18120; Acts 1:8). Yet, in spite of it being a command from our Lord Jesus Himself, disciple-making among both Christian men and Christian women is one of the most neglected areas in church life today. A cursory look at recent articles and surveys on the subject of disciple-making suggests that disciple-making in the contemporary North American church is superficial at best, and non-existent at worst. The results have been described as producing "Jesus namers" rather than "Jesus-followers," Or, as John Stott remarked in a presentation he gave at the church where I am a pastor, "Christianity in America today is 3600 miles wide and an inch deep." Syndicated columnist Cal Thomas underscored this condition in an interview in *Christianity Today* where he observed: "The problem in our culture isn't the abortionists. It isn't the pornographers or drug dealers or criminals; it is the undisciplined, *undiscipled,* disobedient, and Biblically ignorant Church of Jesus Christ" (italics mine).[25] Whom shall we blame for this?

Have you noticed how so many people these days are not willing to take responsibility for their own actions? Blame-shifting is prevalent. Humorist Will Rogers once said that the history of North America would be written in three phases: the passing of the Indian; the passing of the buffalo; and the passing of the buck. Cartoonist Charles Schultz proffered a similar idea in his *Peanuts* cartoon strip. Peppermint Patty telephones Charlie Brown: *"Guess what, Chuck. It was the first day of school and I got sent to the principal's office. It was your fault, Chuck!"* Surprised, Charlie Brown replies, *"MY fault? How could it be MY fault? Why do you always say everything is MY fault?"* Peppermint Patty explains, *"You're my friend, aren't you, Chuck? You should have been a better influence on me!"*

When Jesus called His followers to influence others in the most important way possible—making disciples—He did not want us to pass the buck, but to take responsibility for this precious privilege He gives to every Christian.

Most of us lack a person in our lives who will take us deeper in our knowing and following Christ so that we, in turn, can take someone else deeper. And yet, we are often perplexed by our own lack of growth as Christians and disappointed when we aren't as strong as we believe we should be in the face of temptations or the trials of life. In addition, we often are frustrated by how quickly young people stray from the faith when they go away to college or get out on their own. What is lacking is our participation in the strategy Jesus had in mind—making disciples.

Recently, as I was speaking to a group of Christians, I asked for a show of hands as to how many in the group considered themselves to be Christians. Nearly every hand was raised. Then, I asked how many considered themselves to be disciples of Jesus, and the hands quickly came down, indicating to me the disparity that exists in our understanding of what a disciple of Jesus really is. As I interacted with that group, it became apparent that those Christians regarded being a disciple a higher level of spirituality than being just a Christian, and that discipleship was for the spiritually elite, not for the ordinary believer, a view that is not confined to that group, but is prevalent among Christians today. Perhaps it is because we do not have a clear understanding of what a disciple of Jesus is, we have not been discipled ourselves, and consequently, are not participating in the process of making disciples.

What is a Disciple and what is Discipleship?

Simply put, a disciple is a learner, an apprentice; and discipleship is the process of learning from someone by both precept and example and following that person. Every Christian *is* a disciple. Jesus began the process by investing in a few key men He called to follow Him. He then commissioned them to do the same, understanding that if each of them passed on to several others what He had instilled in them, and those others did the same with a few more, and the process continued from generation to generation, the principle of multiplication would result in the exponential spread of the Gospel and both the spiritual and the numerical growth of the Church.

The Apostle Paul reflected his understanding of this strategy when he instructed his protégé, Timothy, *"The things which you have heard from me...entrust these to faithful men who will be able to teach others also"* (2 Timothy 2:2). Yet, being discipled and being a discipler is generally foreign to far too many contemporary Christians.

At the end of 2 Timothy 1, Paul refers to the widespread defection of Christians in that area when the going got tough. In light of this, he saw a gap in the disciple-making process, and the need for the shoring up of Christians in their faith, spiritual grounding and growth to remedy superficial faith and ostensible commitment to Christ. In 2 Timothy 2:1, Paul then urges Timothy to stand against the trends toward mediocrity with these words: "Be strong in the grace that is in Christ Jesus." In other words, never mind what others are doing. *You* stand strong. He then continues with his charge to Timothy to pick up Jesus' disciple-making process by taking the truths of Christ and behaviors that he had learned from Paul and passing them on to other men who could do the same with still others.

This is a precious privilege given to each Christian without exception: to learn about and experience God and His wisdom for living the Christian life, serving Christ, and then to pass this on to a few others. You can see immediately that doing this is in keeping with Christ's great commission to us when He said, *"As you are going along in this world, make disciples...teaching them to do whatever I have commanded you."* Paul had good reason to do so.

In 2 Timothy 1, the Apostle Paul had told Timothy (and us) to guard the Gospel and preserve God's truth. I doubt there is a Christian anywhere who wouldn't want to do that. We want to make sure nobody changes the message of Good News that Jesus Christ the Son of God came to earth, lived this life perfectly—without sin—in complete obedience to God, and then offered that life on the cross as a sacrifice, pouring out His life blood as atonement for our sin. That Jesus was powerfully raised from the dead by God the Father, as the Father accepted Christ's sacrifice as sufficient payment for our sin. Therefore, anyone who puts his faith and trust in Jesus Christ alone, asking for God's forgiveness, will not only be completely pardoned and set right with God, but will receive the gift of eternal life. That is the Gospel. We must guard it. We want to preserve God's truth. There are many Christians who would give their all for the truths we Christians have held dear for centuries. We would make sure that the church does not vary or stray from these. But, if that is all we do, it would last for only a short time. No, more than to simply guard the Gospel and preserve God's great truths as found in the Bible, we must learn to pass them on and on and on.

When he planted the church in Ephesus, the Apostle Paul knew that he would be there only three years. That is why he discipled young Timothy and others in the faith. In fact, Paul describes this process in four stages. First, Christ had entrusted the Gospel and the body of great Biblical truths to Paul, everything necessary for people to know about living this life in a good and godly way. These were not inventions of Paul, but came from Jesus Christ Himself. Next, Paul passed on this heritage of faith and truth by mentoring Timothy and others. Then, Paul urges Timothy to do the same. He is to identify others to whom he can teach the Gospel and Biblical truths for living; others he can mentor; others for whom Timothy can model what it looks like to follow Jesus. Finally, those who are taught by Timothy can, in turn, teach others also. In doing so, the strategy of Jesus' mission is carried out faithfully.

In Titus 2: 3-5, Paul gives similar instruction to the women of the early church: *"Older women likewise are to be reverent in their behavior...*

teaching what is good, so that they may train the young women to love their husbands and children, to be sensible, pure, workers at home, kind...so that the word of God will not be dishonored." In these ways, the torch of God's truth is passed from more mature Christians to growing Christians: fathers to sons, mothers to daughters; men and women a bit farther along in the faith to those who are newer or younger in the faith. Then, as Jesus says in Luke 6: 40, everyone, after he has been fully trained, will be *like* his teacher. Ah, you say, there is the rub. I'm not sure I'm the kind of Christian I would want someone else to be. May I tell you something? Nothing gets a Christian on track better in his own walk with Christ than when he is being a teacher and an example, a discipler to someone else. Furthermore, to relegate the disciple-making process only to those who we regard as "spiritually elite" is to miss some fundamental principles regarding the disciple-making process as adapted from Michael Wilkins by Bill Hull in his book, *The Complete Book of Discipleship:*

"Any residual spiritual elitism can be trumped by some basic tenets regarding discipleship:

- *All* Christians are disciples who are born anew to spiritual life when they choose to follow Jesus.
- Both the starting point and the goal of spiritual formation and discipleship is transformation to the image of Christ.
- Together discipleship and spiritual formation provide a full New Testament perspective of the process of the growth of Christians.

- Spiritual formation and discipleship must be biblically and theologically grounded."[26]

A mistake that is frequently made once a church or a group of Christians realizes that disciple-making is a good and necessary thing is to attempt to institute a discipleship *program* where people go through a published set of discipleship materials for a designated number of weeks or months with a view toward being successfully discipled as the outcome. Some participate. Many don't because it appears to them to be another classroom-type Bible study. That is why it is important for us to realize that, by definition, disciple-making is a *process*, not a program and involves relationships, not just curriculum in a classroom. Greg Ogden makes this distinction and elaborates it in his fine book titled *Transforming Discipleship,* reading I would recommend for any follower of Christ who wishes to better understand and pursue obedience to Christ's call to make disciples. (His companion book, *Discipleship Essentials* is an excellent tool to use within disciple-making relationships.)

In any event, one point is clear. This is *mandatory* disciple-making. I chose the word *mandatory* because the disciple-making process is commanded, first by Jesus, and then by His Apostles. While it is a precious privilege for each of us to pass on our knowledge and experience of God and His truth, it is not optional. In fact, the context of the commands to make disciples, to guard the Gospel, to preserve the truth and pass these on to others, suggests that such a worthwhile ministry will involve counting the cost, inconvenience, sacrifice and, perhaps, even suffering (Luke 14:26-35; 2Timothy 2:3-6). However, the life-transforming effect that disciple-making produces and the resulting growth and multiplication of faithful followers of Christ are well worth it (2 Corinthians 4:17, 18) and guarantee both the spiritual and numerical growth of the Christian community as well. It's a great plan, Christ's master plan for you and me.

Interestingly, when Jesus commissioned His followers shortly before ascending into heaven and sending His Holy Spirit to empower them, He didn't urge them to craft compelling church services or offer a proliferation of attractive programs, or even huddle within the safe confines of church buildings and hold on until He returned. He gave them robust marching orders which have now been passed to us—"Make disciples!" And this is precisely what they and every faithful follower of Christ have done since. That is why, in 1Timothy 2:2, the Apostle Paul makes certain that one of our central purposes as Christians is clarified: to help someone else follow Jesus, just as you have chosen to follow Jesus. Those who have walked with Christ for awhile can take someone else under wing and mentor him or her in the faith. It seems like people with a passion to follow Christ themselves, have a passion to obey His commission to make disciples, to mentor others, bringing people to the point of being fully devoted, Christ-centered followers of Jesus.

At this point, I feel compelled to make a distinction. Jesus did NOT say, "Make converts." He said, "Make disciples." Perhaps our reconstruction of the Gospel of Jesus Christ, making it a message of how to get your sins forgiven so that you can go to heaven one day, rather than one that calls us to be reconciled to God through Christ's death and resurrection so that we can get into Jesus' life in a way that transforms ours, has allowed us to settle for securing converts to Christ rather than making disciples of Christ. The difference is significant. A convert might pray a prayer to accept Jesus as his Savior and be left with the impression that he is now eternally safe and secure and can get on with his life. Of course he should attend church, read his Bible, and perhaps serve God in some way. But since none of these is necessary for his salvation, they become optional considerations to be carried out at his convenience. However, a disciple is someone who, being converted to Christ, grows to maturity in Christ because someone else invests in "teaching him to do everything [Christ] has commanded" in a disciple-making relationship. As a result of this process, the gap between those who become Christians but experience little growth and those who become fully devoted, Christ-centered Christ-followers is closed.

So the questions must be pressed: "Have you or are you being discipled by someone else?" And, "To whom are you teaching the things of Christ so that they may be able to teach others also?" Who are you mentoring? For whom are you modeling a faithful walk with Christ? Inherent in Christ's call on our lives is a call to mandatory mentoring, disciple-making, the high privilege of intentionally passing on to others what we have been taught and what we have learned in our walk with God. It is a call to every Christian, bar none. And, as is always true of God's commands, what He prescribes is always what is best. Therefore, we can say to Him, "I want to do what you have prescribed because I trust you and know that the experience and results will be positive, not only for me, but for others as well." Just think of what it would mean if every Christian began to have relationships with other Christians in two directions: one where we ourselves are receiving teaching from another who is discipling us and modeling a faithful walk with Christ for us; and one where we are passing on what we have learned and experienced of Christ to another, and encouraging that person to do the same with still another. Can you see the genius of Christ's discipling, reproduction plan for His church? Can you see how crucial it is that all of us engage in this process, especially for the sake of the next generation of Christians? Actually, there is another benefit in all of this. As I mentioned earlier, you never learn God's truth as well as when you are teaching it to another. Christians who mentor others typically grow dramatically themselves.

Sometimes we measure what we are presently doing by what we have always done before and by what our experience in the church has been previously. Perhaps we have never been discipled personally by someone else. We, in turn, have never mentored another. So we tend to repeat this pattern, feeling that we are all getting by that way. But we can see from the Scriptures that God has a better way. He has told us that this is what He wants us to do, to learn of Him, grow in the faith, and to be intentional about personally passing on God's truth to others who will be faithful to teach others also. It is basic to Christian living.

When former Green Bay Packers' coach Vince Lombardi, in frustration after his team's mediocre play, held up that oblong leather object and said, "Gentlemen, this is a football," he was being both facetious and serious. The players had gotten away from the fundamentals of the game, and needed desperately to return to those first principles. Christian disciple-making is basic Christianity. It is foundational to our progress, growth and success.

In any given church, there are people all along the path of spiritual growth. There are relatively new believers who are in need of those who are farther down the road of faith. There are young people who need older Christians to teach and model a life of following hard after Christ. While small groups, growth groups, life groups and the like are important venues for Christian relationships, they are no substitute for mentoring relationships. Opportunities and needs abound for smaller and more intimate Christian disciple-making relationships. Will you enter in? If you feel inadequate and not mature enough in your own faith, ask God to direct you to someone else who can begin to mentor you. Then, look at people in your church to whom you would be willing to entrust your spiritual care. Or check in with your pastor to see whom he might recommend. He may be able to connect you with a suitable person who has already indicated an interest and willingness to be a discipler. Once you've identified a potential mentor, ask that person if he or she would consider a discipleship relationship with you. If they agree, you'll be on your way. After some time in that relationship, you will want to be sharing with someone else what you are learning and experiencing. If every one of us seizes this precious privilege of mandatory mentoring, and determines to connect with someone who can disciple us and also with someone we can disciple for Christ, it will make a significant difference in our own lives and in the future of the Church of Jesus Christ.

CHAPTER TEN:

ENGAGING IN HIS REGIMEN

Annie Dillard wrote, "How we spend our days, is how we spend our lives." How are you spending your days? Your life? When you come to the end of your life, do you think you will be satisfied? Will you have a sense that you have done what God intended for you?

As we consider the mission to which Jesus calls us, a life of rigorously following Him, and of extending loving compassion to the oppressed and needy, and as we participate in the strategy He put in place—to make disciples—we are pressed to ask, "Where will I find the time, the energy and the internal resources to carry this out?" There is an essential prerequisite that is apparent in the life and daily habits of our Lord. Some call it "soul care."

At the end of His life, Jesus could say to God His Father, *"I have accomplished the work you gave Me to do."* Will you be able to say the same? At the close of his days, the Apostle Paul, who knew what it meant to get into Jesus' life, wrote, *"I have fought a good fight, I have completed the course, I have kept the faith. Therefore, a reward awaits me."* Will you say that too? Or do you feel like life is on overload, that there isn't enough time to do everything you want to do, or have to do, or ought to do? And even if there was enough time, you wouldn't be able to handle it all anyway. You who are students know what I mean. There are classes, homework, chores, jobs, sports, recreation, church activities, things you want to learn to do, and opportunities you don't want to miss. For all of us, it seems that between work, family responsibilities, projects, interests, church activities, calamities and other things that go wrong, unfinished tasks, unread books, unwritten correspondence, unfulfilled good intentions—we feel overwhelmed. Life seems so busy and so cluttered. For some, it feels out of control. Not surprisingly, an issue of *Newsweek* carried a cover story titled, "Exhausted." In it, medical doctor Richard A. Swenson writes: "The spontaneous tendency of our culture is to inexorably add detail to our lives: one more option, one more problem, one more commitment, one more expectation, one more purchase, one more debt, one more change, one more job, one more decision. We must now deal with more 'things per person' than at any other time in history. Yet one can comfortably handle only so many details in his or her life. Exceeding this threshold will result in disorganization or frustration. It is important to note here that the problem is not in the 'details'; the problem is in the 'exceeding.' This is called overloading."[27]

Jesus did not live this way. Nor is it necessary for us to live this way either. After all, Jesus has called us to deny ourselves, get into His life, and become like Him. Effective Christian living begins by understanding the goal: *to be conformed to the image of God's Son* (Romans 8: 29). To put it another way, God reconciles us to Himself through the sacrifice of His Son, in order to restore His likeness in us. We are to become like Jesus. As Dallas Willard asserts in his book *The Spirit of the Disciplines:* "My central claim is that we *can* become like Christ by doing one thing—by following him in the overall style of life he chose for himself. If we have faith in Christ, we must believe that he knew how to live. We can, through faith and grace, become like Christ by practicing the types of activities he engaged in, by arranging our whole lives around the activities he himself practiced in order to remain constantly at home in the fellowship of his Father."[28] In other words, we engage in Jesus' spiritual regimen, trading the myriad drives and desires that result in our own cluttered agendas, for the straightforward, single-minded purpose of pursuing our Savior and being like Him.

Webster defines *regimen* as a system of control or discipline usually pertaining to exercise, therapy or diet intake. To put it in the Apostle Paul's words, we *"discipline [ourselves] for the purpose of godliness"* (1 Timothy 4:7).

A person does not *try* to run a marathon; he *trains* to run that race. Nor does a person try to be a virtuoso violinist or a skilled surgeon. He trains for these as well. Yet, we expect to achieve virtuoso Christianity by trying, not training. We cannot. We must train by engaging in Christ's regimen of a spiritually disciplined life, one day at a time, one step at a time, for a lifetime. By following Christ, we learn the secret to a God-centered life. Jesus set a perfect example for us by tending to His inner life, keeping priorities straight, and removing unnecessary clutter. He could not imagine a love relationship without the investment of time to commune with the object of His love and to cultivate intimacy. Getting into His life, we discover His secret recounted in the record of His ministry, the Gospels.

Jesus Made Prayer a Priority

"When evening had come, after the sun had set, they began bringing to him all who were ill and those who were demon-possessed. And the whole city had gathered at the door. And He healed many who were ill with various diseases, and cast out many demons.... And in the early morning, while it was still dark, He arose and went out and departed to a lonely place, and was praying there. Simon and his companions hunted for Him; and they found Him and said to Him, 'Everyone is looking for you.' And He said to them, 'Let us go somewhere else to the towns nearby, in order that I may preach there also; for that is what I came out for.' And He went into their synagogues throughout all Galilee, preaching and casting out the demons" (Mark 1:32-39).

Jesus did not live his life arbitrarily, but purposefully. He was not ruled by the tyranny of the urgent, but was directed by His Father's will. In John 14:10, Jesus says, *"I am in the Father, and the Father is in Me. The words that I say to you I do not speak on My own initiative, but the Father abiding in Me does His works."* Imagine living like that. Jesus was directed because He was connected. Yes, even for the Son of God, prayer was essential for His life of perfect obedience to His heavenly Father. It was His necessary connection to knowing His heavenly Father's will.

Remember that Jesus became like us when He came to earth. He voluntarily laid aside and restricted His divine prerogatives so that, like us, He would be totally dependent on God the Father through the indwelling Holy Spirit in His daily life and ministry. Just as Jesus says to us, "Apart from Me you can do nothing," the same was true regarding Jesus with respect to His relationship with God His Father. It was through prayer that Jesus maintained and sustained an intimate association with His heavenly Father. Prayer was not simply a religious exercise. It was the necessary means by which Jesus fixed His loving gaze on His Father and bonded with Him. Through prayer, Jesus consulted God the Father and tapped into His Father's wisdom, power and guidance. As a result, Jesus had a remarkable sense of priority, calmness and balance. Even though He had to work hard and experienced opposition, calamity, struggles, suffering and enormous demands on His time and gifts, Jesus lived a clutter-free life. The external world did not determine or run His life. That is because He tended to the first and most important matter—His inner life, His relationship to His Heavenly Father.

In the passage from the Gospel of Mark above, we see the whole city clamoring at Jesus' door pressing Him for His compassionate, healing ministry, something that to us would appear to be of highest priority. Yet, instead of reacting to that demand, Jesus takes time for solitude, prayer, meditation and reflection. In the middle of His heaviest, most demanding schedule, helping people late into the night, we find Jesus, not sleeping in the next day, but getting up before sunrise so that he could take time to be alone with God the Father and pray. While it may seem odd to us that Jesus would put His teaching, helping, and healing ministry on hold when so many were in need of Him, He realized that He simply could not continue effectively without soul-nurturing, resource-restoring prayer.

Jesus understood something He wants us to know right now—that prayerful communing with God in a quiet place where we will not be disturbed, is indispensable to productive living and effective service. In the quiet place of prayer, Jesus was refreshed from the taxing stress of being involved with people's problems and ministering to their needs day in and day out. In the quiet place of prayer, He set His priorities so that His life and His energies were spent sensibly and efficiently. In this way, He tuned in to His Father's Word and will. From that vantage point, with the direction of the Holy Spirit to Whom He was fully yielded, Jesus could make the tough choices that kept His life from becoming cluttered with unnecessary stuff and going into overload. He could both know and choose to do exactly what God the Father intended.

Given the response and the size of the crowd, the disciples were ready to pitch a tent, put up billboards and run an ad campaign that Jesus would be extending His evangelistic meetings in that area. They were ready to set the agenda for Jesus. You know how it goes, "God loves you and everybody else has a plan for your life!" But Jesus found His direction early in the morning in that place of quiet solitude, alone with His father. He stayed spiritually connected to his Heavenly Father through prayer and the Word. Consequently, He was continually strengthened and directed by His Father moment by moment.

In the writings of Isaiah, we find a prophetic portrait of the Servant of the Lord, the coming Messiah, Jesus Christ, describing this dimension of His relationship with God the Father.

"The Lord God has given Me the tongue of disciples, that I may know how to sustain the weary one with a word. He awakens Me morning by morning. He awakens My ear to listen as a disciple. The Lord God has opened My ear, and I was not disobedient, nor did I turn back. I gave My back to those who strike Me, and My cheeks to those who pluck out the beard; I did not cover My face from humiliation and spitting. For the Lord God helps Me. Therefore, I am not disgraced; Therefore, I have set My face like flint, and I know that I shall not be disappointed. He who vindicates Me is near..." (Isaiah 50:4-8).

Jesus was focused. He refused to let the external world set His agenda. He ordered His priorities in the quiet times of prayer and reflection on God's Word and, at all cost, stuck to the decisions He made there. He stood firm, trusting God the Father with the outcomes because He was taking His directions from His Father who says so clearly, *"Those who honor me, I will honor"* (1 Samuel 2:30).

Jesus knew and trusted in His Father's love for Him. The beauty, power and effectiveness of Jesus' life flowed out of His vital connection to His Father through prayer. Prayer must never be merely a drug for our frenzy or a medicine for our emergency. Prayer is the avenue by which we seek God and grow in our intimate knowing of Him. It is by communing with God in the quiet place of prayer that we learn to call him "Abba," "Daddy," "Dear Father." As we commune with the Lord in prayer and listen for His voice in His Word, He frees us from the tyranny of the urgent. He enables us to choose to do the things that *He*, not we, has determined are most important, things *He* wants us to accomplish. He impresses upon us the assignments *He* wants us to undertake. When God's directions determine our activities, our activities become powerful and effective. And we don't burn out. We discover what God has in mind and we begin to experience His desires for our lives. In fact, taking time to get alone and pray this way was so important to Jesus, that in chapter 6 of Mark's Gospel,

Jesus Teaches His First Disciples and Us to Make Prayer a Priority As Well

In verses 12, 13, the disciples are serving Christ just as he had directed them:

"They went out and preached that men should repent. And they were casting out many demons and were anointing with oil many sick people and healing them."

Verses 30-32 tell us what happened when they returned to Jesus:

"The apostles gathered together with Jesus, and they reported to Him all that they had done and taught. And He said to them, 'Come away by yourselves to a lonely place and rest a while.' (For there were many people coming and going, and they did not even have time to eat.) And they went away in the boat to a lonely place by themselves."

Do you see it? Again, in the wake of great busyness and the prospect of more ministry to people than all thirteen of them could possibly do, Jesus shows His disciples and us what must happen in spite of the busyness, or perhaps, because of the busyness. *"Come apart before you come apart—at the seams!"* Jesus calls them to a "lonely place," that place of solitude, where they could talk out loud to God and listen for His voice within without distraction. As Henri Nouwen points out, "The discipline of solitude…is one of the most powerful disciplines in developing a prayerful life. It is a simple, though not easy, way to free us from the slavery of our occupations and preoccupations and to begin to hear the voice that makes all things new."[29] For me, that place is a small screened porch next to a lovely garden my wife has planted. It is fragrant and quiet, except for the delicate songs of nearby birds. There in prayer, with my Bible open, I meet with my Lord, listen for His voice, and share my innermost thoughts with Him. It is there that I nurture my soul in His presence. Do you have such a place? Would we find you there often?

Unfortunately, the crowds saw where Jesus and His disciples were going and ran to intercept them, getting to the destination before they did. The disciples didn't get a chance to rest or to pray. You might say that their time of quiet solitude for rest and prayer was literally *crowded* out. They became frustrated and wanted to send the people away. Yet, because it was Jesus' habit and pattern to take the time to pray, He still had power to effectively minister to the people's needs even though this particular prayer time was interrupted. Instead of being annoyed by the crowd, as were His prayerless disciples, Jesus, with a sense of calm priority, is filled with compassion. In a demonstration of the power of His prayer-filled life, Jesus takes five loaves of bread and two fish and miraculously feeds over 5,000 people—with food left over! Jesus dared to attempt God's dreams for Him because He had connected with his Father in prayer. He possessed the discernment to choose wisely, to appropriate His time with proper priority. All too frequently, we come to God with some pending decision or daunting dilemma only to become frustrated or disappointed by a lack of instant clarity or immediate divine response according our wishes; when, if we had engaged in Jesus' regimen and practiced His habits of prayer, we would already possess the necessary wisdom to make the in-the-moment decision. In fact, we may venture further in understanding that God rarely seems to give "instant-answer" responses in order that we would spend regular and extended times of seeking Him in prayer, rather than simply calling out to Him when life presses us or there is something we want from Him. By engaging in Jesus' regimen of communing with our heavenly Father in prayer, we will cultivate the relationship that refreshes us and builds into us the spiritual reserves we need to follow Him.

Now look at the very next thing that Jesus does.

"And immediately He made His disciples get into the boat and go ahead of Him to the other side to Bethsaida, while He Himself was sending the multitude away. And after bidding them farewell, He departed to the mountain to pray." (Mark 6:45, 46)

Jesus never rested on the laurels of past success. Daring to dream, daring to follow His heavenly Father's plans meant moving on. Moving on with a sense of priority and power meant staying spiritually connected and directed. And that meant praying. Will that message get through to us today in a life-changing, habit-forming way? I ask that because, for all my Christian life I have read and heard and even preached urgent messages on how critical prayer is to staying spiritually connected and for genuinely following and obeying Christ. I have heard all God's people say "Amen" to the emphasis that fervent, persistent prayer is absolutely essential to victorious Christian living and to embracing Christ's mission of compassionate service effectively. Yet, today there remains a large prayer deficit in the lives of far too many of us. And I have to ask, will tomorrow be different? Will our programs continue to be full while our prayer meetings remain empty? Or will this affirmation from God's Word on the vitality of prayer in Jesus' life and the necessity of prayer in our own turn the tide? Will we be getting into Jesus' life by engaging in His regimen, the holy habit of talking with the Father in prayer and hearing Him speak to us through His Spirit and His Word?

Perhaps by observing what happens to the prayerless disciples, we will be convinced, because we often see so much of ourselves in them. Remember that they had just returned from serving Christ on a short-term mission trip. He called them aside to rest and be renewed in the quiet place of reflection and prayer. But the crowd cut them off. After that, while Jesus made certain to get alone again to pray, they did not. Just like going without food and water drains us of physical vitality, prayerlessness or minimum praying leaves us spiritually depleted and weak. Suddenly, the disciples find themselves in the middle of a storm on the sea.

"And when it was evening, the boat was in the midst of the sea, and Jesus was alone on the land. And seeing them straining at the oars, for the wind was against them, at about the fourth watch of the night, He came to them, walking on the sea; and He intended to pass by them. But when they saw Him walking on the sea, they supposed that it was a ghost, and cried out, for they all saw Him and were frightened. But immediately He spoke with them and said to them. 'Take courage; it is I, do not be afraid.' And He got into the boat with them, and the wind stopped; and they were greatly astonished..." (Mark 6:47-51).

Sailing into the teeth of strong, adverse winds, Jesus' disciples were straining at the oars. Seeing their dilemma from the shore, Jesus, freshly powered by prayer, walks to them on the water, gets into the boat with them and calms the sea. What is the prayerless disciples' response? First fear, then astonishment. Verse 52 explains their response: *"They had not gained any insight from the incident of the loaves, but their heart was hardened."* Even though they had been eyewitnesses to a miraculous event from the hands of Jesus, the feeding of over 5,000 people with five loaves of bread and two fish, they were bewildered by this incredible sequence of events and slow to believe.

Their response, however, is a mirror in which we see our own likeness. Christians are the recipients of the greatest miracle of all—the new birth to eternal life in Christ. But we are often slow to trust God and to pursue all that He wants to do through us when we connect with Him in prayer. When we do not open our hearts to God in prayer and do not embrace the possibilities, we close our minds to His power. The words *can't* and *impossible* slip into our vocabulary, into our thinking and into our expectations for the impact of our lives on others within our spheres of influence. Without prayer, we are going it on our own. Without prayer, we neither understand nor experience Christ's source of power and direction. The potential of extraordinary spiritual ministry fades into the reality of ordinary human efforts and results. Meager praying or prayerlessness are large obstacles to our daring great things for God and seeing astonishing results. That is why the poet wrote: *Oh you who sigh and languish and mourn your lack of power. Hear His gentle whisper, "Could you not pray with me one hour?" For fruitfulness and blessing, there is no royal road; the power for holy service is intercourse with God.* That intercourse is our fervent praying. But, as the ageless adage asserts, *"You can't have the fruit if you don't climb the tree."*

Knowing the desolation of prayerlessness in a person's life, with characteristic passion, Charles Spurgeon pressed these questions to his congregation, questions we also must answer: "Men and women, let me ask you, 'How long has it been since you have had an intimate conversation with Jesus Christ?' Some of you may be able to say, 'It was only this morning that I last spoke with him; I beheld his face with joy.' But I fear that the great majority of you will have to say, 'It has been months since I have been with the Lord.' What have you been doing with your life? Do not let me condemn you or judge; only let your conscience speak. Have we not all lived too much without Jesus: Have we not grown contented with the world to the neglect of Christ?"[30]

In the Mark 8, Jesus underscores what the disciples and we lack when we pray little or not at all. Again, Jesus has demonstrated how His activities were powered by prayer as He casts out a demon from a child, gives hearing and speech to a deaf and dumb man, and feeds four thousand more people with just seven loaves of bread. Then, in the wake of all this, something happens that reveals the desperate condition of unbelief in prayerless hearts. As we see what happens among those still prayerless disciples, we must be careful not to judge them too quickly. We might find ourselves among them

"They had forgotten to take bread; and did not have more than one loaf in the boat with them. And Jesus was giving orders to them, saying, 'Watch out! Beware of the leaven of the Pharisees and the leaven of Herod.' And they began to discuss with one another the fact that they had no bread. And Jesus, aware of this, said to them, 'why do you discuss the fact that you have no bread? Do you not yet see? And having ears, do you not hear? And do you not remember when I broke the five loaves for the five thousand, how many large baskets full o f broken pieces you picked up?' They said to Him, 'Twelve.' 'And when I broke the seven loaves for the four thousand, how many baskets full of broken pieces did you pick up?' And they said to Him, 'Seven.' And He said to them, 'Do you not yet understand?'" (Mark 8:14-21.)

"Dear disciples," Jesus says to them in frustration, "You still don't get it, do you? No matter how much I've taught you, no matter how much you've seen, no matter how often you've been told, you still don't get it, do you?" I had to stop and ask myself if, today, we Christians get it. Or do we still minimize the role of prayer in our lives and in the church and continue to be the source of our own sufficiency? What do you think? Leonard Ravenhill makes these pointed observations: "The church has many organizers, but few agonizers. Many who pay, but few who pray; many who are enterprising, but few who are interceding." Then he adds, "People who are not praying are playing. Tithes may build a church, but tears will give it life. That is the difference between the modern church and the early church. Our emphasis is on paying. Theirs was on praying. When we have paid, the place is taken. When they had prayed, the place was shaken (Acts 4: 31). In the matter of effective praying, never have so many left so much to so few. Brethren, let us pray."[31]

How can we complain about what we don't have or what we cannot accomplish when Jesus has shown us the possibilities and has revealed to us how to access those possibilities by being spiritually connected, directed and empowered through prayer? Jesus wants us to regard Him as our source of wisdom and power. Jesus longs for us to experience the relationship He had with God the Father through the intimacy of prayer. He desires to direct and empower us through precious times in prayer and in His Word. In Mark 9, when the disciples failed to cast a demon out of a boy, Jesus again shook His head in wonder about their lack of faith. When they asked Him why He succeeded where they had failed, He answers straightforwardly, "Such is accomplished only by prayer and fasting." Do we understand? Getting into His life, we must engage in His regimen to succeed in His mission of compassion and redemption.

Could our own prayerlessness account for the questions frequently asked by Christians—"How can I know God's will?" or "Why can't I sense God's presence?" or "Why do I lack peace, joy and contentment?" Do we have the right to pose such questions if there is a deficit in our praying; if we are not consistently pursuing God through prayer? "Well," you say, "I'd pray more if I had more peace and less chaos in my life: if I sensed God's presence, or felt more spiritual." Yet, isn't the incongruity of that argument a lot like saying, "I'd exercise more if I were in better shape!"? No, I must get the horse in front of the cart. After I had let myself become overweight and sluggish, I began to experience physical limitations that frustrated a desire I had to run in a five kilometer race with my son. As in my previous marathon illustration, I knew I could not *try* to run a 5K. I had to *train* to run a 5K. I had to engage in a regimen that would produce the condition that would permit the run. I began to walk a few miles each day. Soon I added jogging to my walking. Before long, I was jogging the few miles I had been walking as the weight came off and my endurance grew. Then, on a crisp, clear autumn day in October, my son and I ran a five kilometer fund-raising run for the cause of oppressed African women. Faithfully engaging in a fitness regimen paid off. This principle carries over into the spiritual realm as well.

Our spiritual "jogging" may begin by praying simple prayers wherein we simply talk to God in a spirit of gratitude. We get direction for the regimen by acquiring and reading books on prayer by authors such as E.M. Bounds, Wesley Duewel, and Kenneth Boa. Writing out our prayers before offering them to God will keep us focused and clear, while creating a journal by which we can log our progress. And one of the best ways to improve our intercourse with God is to pray His Word, the Bible, by taking a verse or passage of Scripture and memorizing it. Then, having memorized the portion, we personalize it by placing our name in strategic places. For example, I would personalize the very familiar John 3:16 by saying, "For God so loved John Vosnos that He gave His only begotten Son; that if John Vosnos would believe in Him, John Vosnos would not perish, but John Vosnos would have eternal life." Once we have personalized the passage or verse, we can meditate upon it. The Psalmist writes in Psalm one that the genuinely blessed person is one who delights in the Word of God and meditates on it day and night. The Old Testament Hebrew word for meditate literally means, "chew the cud," suggesting the digestive process of a cow that eats, swallows, regurgitates, chews over, swallows again, and repeats the process a couple of more times until the food consumed is fully absorbed. As we memorize, personalize, and meditate on Scripture by ruminating on it, bringing to mind again and again, we can pray those very words, commands, promises, and cautions back to God and grow in our knowing and understanding of His will and ways. It is a regimen by which we will experience spiritual growth and stamina for the most demanding circumstances of life. It is the regimen that served Jesus well.

In Mark 14, we see that through His praying on the eve of His horrible crucifixion and selfless sacrifice for our sins, Jesus attached Himself to the will of God, even though it meant suffering and death. In the Garden of Gethsemane, from the anguish of His soul He prays, "Abba, precious Father! All things are possible for You; remove this cup from Me; yet not what I will, but what You will" (Mark 14:36). Through His faithful regimen in prayer and in the Scriptures, God's Word, Jesus had cultivated such complete trust in His Father's will that whatever came His way, He regarded it as part of God's plan. He knew that the will of God was the love of God. Therefore, it could only be for good, even if the action against Him from others was evil. Have you come to the place where you trust in the Father's love like that? We will get there only by cultivating an intimate trust relationship with God through prayer.

When Jesus came to the end of His life, He cried out from the cross, "It is finished!" By this He indicated that all that the Father called Him to do had been accomplished and completed. No, He didn't finish all the urgent tasks or meet every crying human need pressing in on Him from people all around. He didn't get involved in every educational, vocational or recreational opportunity that came along, as though He would suffer deprivation unless He did. He didn't even worry about how lack of participation in all of these things would look on His resume´. But, He did carry out the extraordinary mission to which God called Him through the power and direction of the Holy Spirit unleashed by prayer.

Jesus has shown us the way. Getting into His life, we embrace His mission of compassion and redemption. To do that successfully, we engage in His life regimen—particularly through prayer and immersion in God's Word. Dear Christian, *we* choose what will be true of us and of our holy habits, of the spending of our days—and our lives. The Bible says, *"Draw near to God and He will draw near to you"* (James 4: 8). Thomas Merton said it well, "We are already united to God. Contemplative prayer brings us into consciousness of what is already there."[32] Nicholas Herman, later known as Brother Lawrence, experienced such a consciousness of God's presence, saying, "I make it my business only to persevere in his holy presence wherein I keep myself by simple attention and a general fond regard to God, which I refer to as an *actual presence* of God. Or, to put it another way, an habitual, silent, and secret conversation of the soul with God. This often causes me to have feelings of inward rapture—and sometimes outward ones! They are so great that I am forced to have to moderate them and conceal them from others."[33] In your heart of hearts, do you desire to get into Jesus life, to know God, to walk with Him in love, and have your life directed and powered by His Holy

Spirit? Our Lord didn't say, "Give me a minute or two in the morning and an hour on Sunday and that will be sufficient to connect us." Rather, He urges, "If with *all* your heart you truly seek Me, you shall surely find Me" (Jeremiah 29:13, 14). Remember how, in Luke 10:38-42 we see a well-meaning woman named Martha completely distracted by her busyness and things she thought were more important that spending quiet time with Jesus; and how Jesus had to reprimand her for making lesser things more important in her life? Yet, at the very same time He commended her sister, Mary, for choosing to put necessary margin in her life by setting aside life's busyness to take time to sit at Jesus' feet and commune with Him. Which of these people are we more like? Hasn't Jesus made it clear that if we seek Him, His Kingdom, and His righteousness first, everything else that we deem so important, things that busy and distract us, He will provide? Do we trust Him enough to choose the path to which He is pointing us?

In Luke 18:1ff. Jesus shows us by way of a parable "that at all times [we] should pray and not lose heart." If you are already there and are satisfied with the time you spend and the way you commune with God in prayer and in His Word, keep on with this excellent habit of the heart. You are growing into Christ and in the power of His might. But if you are not happy with the state of your spiritual habits, then today must be the day you choose to engage in Jesus' regimen of solitude, stillness, reflection in God's Word and prayer, and no longer be the source of your own sufficiency. You will find Jesus to be the sanctuary of your soul.

Prayer: *Abba, Father, may you find me daily kneeling at your knee, or crawling into you lap to draw near to you, to trust in your love, and to hear from you your heart's desires for me. May I learn of you and choose your will for my life. Teach me the holy habits of my Lord Jesus, especially in the areas of prayer and soaking in your Word, in order that I may be to the praise of your glory. Amen.*

CHAPTER ELEVEN:

CONTINUING WITH COURAGE

Engaging in Jesus regimen bolsters the courage one needs to continually follow Christ fully and faithfully because it helps us address the *fear factor* and find peace.

I was just seven years old when my older sister came into my room and told me a frightening ghost story she had heard. It really scared me. For the next several nights (if not weeks), I had to sleep with a light on. I was really afraid. Now, as an adult, I can look back and say that there really was nothing to be afraid of. As former president Franklin Roosevelt said so memorably, "There is nothing to fear but fear itself." But, for a seven-year-old boy, that was enough. Yet, even as an adult, I find that there are plenty of things in life to cause one's anxiety level to rise. Fear of an uncertain future in a society that in some ways is breaking down. Fear of living an insignificant life. Fear of rejection—of not being accepted by certain people or groups. Fear of failure in my job, my parenting, my finances. Fear of sickness, aging and death. Fear for my children and the things that threaten them. On that note, *Newsweek* some time ago covered stories that included these titles: "America's Nuclear Secrets," "Breast Cancer Gene," "Violent Rap," "How to Survive a Scary Market," "A Children's Diary of War," and "Shattered," which had to do with earthquakes and other natural disasters. At the heart of each of these articles was a single seed—fear. Researchers at Johns Hopkins University reported that forty years ago, the greatest fears of grade school children were animals, being in a dark room, high places, strangers and loud noises. Today, kids are afraid of divorce, nuclear war, cancer, pollution, and being mugged or killed.

In addition to things we fear might happen to us, there are those fears that keep us from attempting things we should (even something as simple as sharing our faith in Christ with others). No, I am no longer a seven-year-old who sleeps with the light on. But can I really say there is nothing to fear but fear itself? Can I say that to the man with a family to support who has just lost his job? Or to the woman who has just been diagnosed with breast cancer? Or to the student who is going to a new and strange school for the first time? Or to the wife whose husband has just left her a single parent with two children? Or to the parent whose child has just run away? Nothing to fear but fear?

Do you know what one phrase from God is repeated in the Bible more than any other? "Fear not." "Fear not" is spoken repeatedly by prophets, apostles, martyrs, angels, and by Christ Himself—all of whom learned by experience that when your life is connected to God's by faith, there is, in fact, nothing to fear but fear itself. In fact, "fear not" is at the heart of what Jesus teaches us in John 16 as we listen in on His final instructions to his disciples while He Himself faces a most fearful experience, His crucifixion on a Roman cross just outside the city walls of Jerusalem.

In summary, these people had chosen to follow Jesus, just as so many of us have. In doing so, they understood that there might be some degree of uncertainty and risk. They had no idea. They said that they believed in Him, just as we say. But their world was about to fall apart. Fear would overtake them. A sense of failure, loss and desperation would overwhelm them. Anxiety would bring to them that sick, tight feeling in the middle of the chest or pit of the stomach. But, before all this happens, Jesus shares with them a secret. It is in John 16:33: *"...that in Me you may have peace."* "Oh yes," Jesus adds, "in this world, in this life, bad stuff will happen that could cause fear, anxiety, worry, concern, even terror. But take courage. I have overcome all of it (and *in Me*, so can you!)"

In the farewell message that Jesus gives to his first followers and now to us in John 13-16, Jesus makes it clear that, although He is leaving this earth physically, He is not leaving us on our own. He gives us the Holy Spirit Who is not only with us, but lives within us (John 14:17), giving us God's presence and power at all times. Speaking to perplexed disciples who could not understand why He had to leave, Jesus quietly responds to their need, not to their question.

"Jesus knew that they wished to question Him, and He said to them, 'Are you deliberating together about this, that I said, 'A little while, and you will not behold Me, and again a little while, and you will see me'? Truly, truly I say to you, that you will weep and lament but the world will rejoice; you will be sorrowful, but your sorrow will be turned to joy. Whenever a woman is in labor, she has sorrow, because her hour has come; but when she gives birth to the child, she remembers the anguish no more, for joy that a child has been born into the world. Therefore you, too, now have sorrow; but I will see you again, and your heart will rejoice, and no one takes your joy away from you." (John 16:19-22)

Jesus indicates that anguish and pain well may be part and parcel of living life as His follower in this fallen world without His physical presence. But the pain will be forgotten when the joy is realized. He compares it to a woman who has gone through a difficult labor for the joy of giving birth to a precious child. The reward realized is worth the pain endured. Notice that Jesus does not end on notes of sorrow. This is the fountainhead of hope that sees us through our deepest trials and testing. Jesus showed them then and now shows us how this works in reality. His cross was the source of greatest suffering and eventually, death. But the sorrow did not last. With the resurrection came joy unspeakable and Christ's exaltation. The writer of the book of Hebrews encourages us to run our life race with endurance by pointing us to Jesus. He writes, "Set your focus on Jesus…who, for the joy set before Him, endured the cross, despising the shame, and has sat down at the right hand of the throne of God. Consider Him…so that you may not grow weary and lose heart" (Hebrews 12: 2, 3).

As we saw earlier in the beautiful relationship analogy of the vine and the branches, Jesus again stresses the importance of the Christian's prayer life and *complete dependence* on Him. "Truly, truly I say to you, if you shall ask the Father for anything in My name, He will give it to you. Until now you have asked for nothing in My name; ask, and you will receive, that your joy may be made full" (John 16: 23, 24). This remarkable promise is rooted in the profound truth that follows in verse 27. "The Father Himself loves you, because you have loved Me, and have believed that I came forth from the Father." To this, the disciples respond quite confidently, "Now you are speaking plainly, and are not using a figure of speech. Now we know that You know all things, and have no need for anyone to question You; by this we believe that You came from God" (John 16:29, 30).

Sometimes we *talk* a good game, don't we? Like them, we say boldly in an expression of confidence or a confession of faith, "We believe!" But Jesus is not deceived by this show of confidence. "Jesus answered them, 'Do you now believe? Behold, an hour is coming, and has already come, for you to be scattered, each to his own home, and to leave Me alone; and yet I am not alone, because the Father is with Me" (verses 31, 32).

Jesus is saying to them, "I see an inadequacy in your faith. There is a gaping hole in your confession and confidence. Your spoken faith lacks the quality of being tested, yet standing firm in fearful situations." The faith of these first followers, like ours, is destined for serious testing almost immediately. Jesus predicts that in the face of fear, they will run, they will fold, and they will abandon Him. He quickly points out that such a fearful response, no matter how distressing the circumstance, is totally unnecessary. Nevertheless, they will be scattered. In the face of fear, they will not believe as they could or should. They will, for a time, return to their self-centered, anxiety-filled ways of living. Yet, in spite of their shortcomings, in spite of the fact that they will leave Him in the lurch when the chips are down, Jesus loves them. Don't ever forget that. You may disappoint the Lord from time to time. But that will never separate you from His intense love for you. You can believe in and trust with abandon His love for you.

Jesus says to them, "You will leave Me all alone to face my most serious trial, suffering and death by myself. But, actually, I am not alone. My Father is with Me." In this short statement, Jesus speaks volumes to us as He unfolds the secret for overcoming fear and discovering his joy and peace. Even though Jesus was completely rejected and abandoned by those closest to Him, and in that circumstance had every reason to be full of fear and dread since the ordeal of His cross was just ahead for Him, His chief resource was not his friends. His chief resource was not tranquil circumstances. His chief resource was not even His own determination. His chief resource and sustaining strength came from His Heavenly Father into Whose hands He had willingly placed his destiny. He knew that whatever His Heavenly Father allowed in His life, the Father could be trusted. Peter would later write, "Jesus kept entrusting Himself to the One Who judges righteously..." (1 Peter 2:23). Consequently, Jesus did not worry or fear. He experienced peace of mind and heart, sustained and comforted by the certainty that His Father loved Him and was with him through it all. Undoubtedly, Jesus could recite with assurance those words of confidence from Psalm 23, "Even though I walk through the valley of the shadow of death, I will fear no evil, for you, Lord, are with me." Even as He writhed on the cross on the threshold of death, Jesus commended Himself into His Father's strong hands for His good keeping. In this way, Jesus teaches us that Christians can always count on the presence of God with them. Whenever we fear or feel alone, whether by loss through the death of a loved one or the desertion of spouse or friends, or because of persecution for our faith or whatever, we are never really alone. Jesus, Who Himself promised us, "I will never leave you nor forsake you," assures us of God the Father's loving presence and gracious care at all times and in every circumstance.

In verse 33, Jesus explains that He is sharing all of this with His disciples and us for a very specific purpose—"that *in Me* you may have peace." Do you know this peace? Jesus' intention is our peace. Of course the key phrase here is *in Me*. The condition for such peace is our getting into Jesus' life. Remember what Jesus taught us in the vineyard analogy of the vine and the branches? "Apart from Me, you can do nothing."

For Jesus, the peace He is offering us is not some idealistic fantasy. He offers this peace in the context of reality by adding, "In the world you *will* have tribulation, but take courage, I have overcome the world." Every person must live his life *in this world.* That will involve hard times and tribulation. But not every person will live that life *in Christ,* that is, in a life-giving relationship to Christ by faith in Jesus as Lord of all. It is the life *in Christ* that experiences this peace.

Earlier in the evening that He spoke these words, Jesus promised peace. In John 14:27, He describes it this way: "Peace I leave with you. My peace I give unto you. Not as the world gives do I give to you. Let not your heart be troubled. Neither let it be afraid." Jesus wants us to understand that the peace that the world offers is external—tranquil circumstances, distraction through entertainment, the calming effects of music, the false security of money, psychotherapy, and even the sedation of alcohol and drugs. But the peace that Jesus gives is from within, springing from a relationship with Him resulting in calmness and confidence in God and His purposes in our lives because He loves us and we trust Him. Jesus gives *effectual* peace within by the presence of the Comforter, the Holy Spirit, and the assurance of His care for our well being. The peace that Jesus gives does not consist in the absence of troubles, dangers or threats, but in the presence of God. This peace of mind and heart is not dependent on circumstances or artificial, temporary means of coping or escape. As Jesus spoke of this peace in the face of serious testing, He was fully aware of the stressful suffering and impending death confronting Him that very hour. Still, He had such confidence in the purposes and power of God His Father, and such trust in His Father's love for Him, that He moved forward without hesitation to meet His crisis without fear. This is the kind of peace Jesus willingly gives to us. That is why in John 14: 1, He confidently urges us, "Let not your heart be troubled; believe in God. Believe also in me."

Again, Jesus is realistic. He says we will have tribulation in this world—experiences guaranteed to produce fear. *"Take courage, be of good cheer, fear not,"* Jesus encourages us, *"I have overcome the world."* How incongruous it is for Jesus to say this, given the reality of the cross where His enemies would put Him to death and believe that they had dealt Him total defeat. Yet, Jesus sees the cross itself as the very means to His complete victory over all that this fallen world could do to Him and over the greatest enemies and fear-mongers, Sin and Death. For Jesus, peace of mind and victory was not in getting out of His difficulty, but in going through it and overcoming it with unshakable confidence in the promises of God. His death was the necessary prelude to His resurrection. And when He had overcome even death, that victory would kindle in His followers a worry-free fearlessness that would stand up to anything.

As Jesus is talking to His followers about all of this, sorrow is already overtaking them (John 16:22). Later, that sorrow would deepen into thorough frustration and disillusionment when they saw Him hanging and dying on that Roman cross. Nevertheless, their sorrow did, in fact, turn to joy when He appeared to them resurrected from the dead. Jesus Christ's resurrection from the dead declared to them with power that Jesus is God the Son (Romans 1:4) and confirmed for them everything He had said and promised.

Jesus did leave them physically in His ascension into heaven, but with the assurance that He will come again (Acts 1:1-11). They would rivet their hope in that certainty, even as we must. They would experience suffering and severe trials of every sort as they lived for Christ in this fallen and hostile world. Nevertheless, they would face down their fears with the courage to which He called both them and us. They would, at every turn, experience the peace that He gave them within. They did not lose the joy of which He had spoken. In fact, historians report that for every Christian that was torn apart by lions or slaughtered by gladiators in the first century Roman Coliseum, thirty or more people came to faith in Christ among the spectators in the stands. Why? They saw the calm and peaceful demeanor of these Christians in the face of brutal injury and death. What might today's spectators see in us? God speaks to us in our tribulation, and He speaks to others in our response to it. He has made possible our fearless response because of the victory of Christ.

God's dream for those who get into Jesus' life and follow Him is that they be a people who are not afraid, whose hearts resonate with the declaration of Psalm 27: "The Lord is my light and my salvation; whom then shall I fear? The Lord is the strength of my life. Of whom shall I be afraid?" And whose courage is bolstered by the charge of the Lord in Joshua 1:9, "Be strong and of good courage; do not be afraid or dismayed; for I, the Lord your God, am with you wherever you go." Today, such fearlessness is a reality in the lives of so many Christians around the world who are literally suffering and dying because of their identity with Jesus Christ. By looking at their lives in a time contemporary to ours, we can learn from them how to stop fearing and to trust in God's love for us.

Many of these stories are told in an intense collection produced by the Christian musical group, *dc Talk* and The Voice of the Martyrs Ministry titled, *Jesus Freaks: Martyrs* (Bethany House, May 2005). During China's *Red Guard* era, two Christian girls, Chiu Chin Hsiu and Ho Hsiu Tzu were threatened with death if they did not recant their faith in Jesus Christ. When they refused, the gun that would kill them was placed in their pastor's hands. He was promised release from prison if he would execute them. The girls' courage, fueled by their unrelenting trust in Christ, stood in marked relief against their pastor's fear which moved him to fire the fatal shots, after which he himself was betrayed by his captors and shot to death anyway. In Indonesia, a young teen-age boy named Roy Pontoh was attending a Christian Bible camp with other young people when angry Muslims invaded their meeting, forced Roy to stand up in front of all and threatened his life if he did not renounce Jesus Christ. Bravely, with unflinching faith in His Savior, Roy refused them. His attackers hacked his body open with a sword and dumped his lifeless body in a nearby ditch. These fully devoted followers of Christ and so many, many more like them had come to know and to trust in God's love for them and held firmly to the happy certainty they had in the promises of their Savior. They displayed the reality that "perfect love casts out fear" (1 John 4:18).

As I read these accounts, I thought of Emily Bronte's brief, but poignant poem:

> "No coward soul is mine,
> No trembler in the world's
> storm-troubled sphere:
> I see the Heaven's
> glories shine,
> and *faith* shines equal,
> arming me from *fear*."

In the book of Revelation, our risen and glorified Lord Jesus Christ through His Apostle John commends the Christians in ancient Smyrna for their fierce and loving loyalty and triumphant spirit over hardship and the severe persecution they incurred because of their faith in Christ whom they loved and followed without wavering. For them, following Jesus was not a "pick and choose" Christianity, or a Christianity of convenience. Their loyalty was rooted in convictions for which they were willing to die. Jesus says to them, "I know your tribulation, your serious trouble. I know your poverty—your following me has cost you dearly. Your possessions have been seized and your employment taken away. You have been stripped of everything and have suffered terribly at the hands of your persecutors. Yet, you have remained faithful. This I promise you: be faithful unto death, and I will give you a crown of life" (Revelation 2:8-10, my paraphrase). Hold on my child. Suffering lasts for a nighttime; but joy comes in the morning!

Getting into Jesus' life, we too can approach Christian living with unusual boldness because of our unshakable confidence in Him, in His love for us and the promise He has made to *"cause all things to work together for good to those who love Him and are called according to His purpose"* (Romans 8:28). Whatever you are presently experiencing, whatever is still to come for you, what was true then, remains true today: "There is nothing to fear but fear itself." Jesus has made it clear: "Fear not, I have overcome the world." And casting all my cares and anxieties on Him, I experience for myself what He intended: "I have said these things to you that *in Me,* you may have peace."

Prayer: *Precious Lord, you have loved me with an everlasting love. I trust in your love for me. You have dressed me in the righteousness of my Lord Jesus. Therefore, I have peace like a river of deep, untroubled waters, comfort immeasurable, joy inexpressible, and confidence that no matter what comes my* *way, my life and times are in your strong and caring hands. I have absolutely nothing to fear. Thank you. Amen.*

CHAPTER TWELVE:

RUNNING AND FINISHING WELL

At the front of a seminary cafeteria line a sign was posted over a bowl of apples: "Please take only one apple. Remember, God is watching!" At the other end of the line was a large container of cookies where a student had posted another sign: "Take all the cookies you want—God is busy watching the apples at the other end." Of course, we know God isn't limited to one end of the cafeteria line. But isn't it true that often we are motivated to do or not to do something by who is watching?

In the summer of A.D. 2004, the Olympic Games returned to their historic birthplace in Athens, Greece. Imagine yourself participating. You are standing in the center of the stadium; but instead of present day athletes parading in, the opening procession is filled with great gold medal winners of the past—Eric

Liddell, Jesse Owens, Bob Matthias, Bob Richards, Wilma Rudolph, Olga Corbett, Mark Spitz, and on and on. Then, instead of staying on the field to participate, they move into the stands and the whole stadium is filled with Olympic greats of the past to cheer *you* on! What a thrill! What encouragement! You begin to feel your adrenaline flow. *They* are watching *you*, and you are charged up and motivated to do your best, because the spectators are those who worked hard, sacrificed greatly, did their very best, and won the gold! In a sense, that is the picture painted for us in Hebrews 12:1:

"Therefore, since we have so great a cloud of witnesses surrounding us, let us also lay aside every encumbrance, and the sin which so easily entangles us, and let us run with endurance the race that is set before us...."

The setting is a race to be won. Based on the phrase *run with endurance*, the race is probably a marathon. The "cloud of witnesses" is the crowd filling the stadium or along the marathon route. But this is not just any crowd. The first word in verse 1, "therefore," sends us back into Hebrew 11 where we find that great "hall of faith," past champions of the faith whose trust in God with abandon was displayed in their self-denial, their persistence, their achievements, their dreadful suffering, and their victories. The writer tells us to remember and to draw encouragement from them in our own run in life. They are called "witnesses" because their lives give testimony to the possibilities of a life of faith. The New Testament word translated *witnesses* is the Greek word *marturas* from which we get the word martyr. This is an appropriate choice of words since the witnesses' obedience to God resulted not only in suffering, but often in death. As we look at them surrounding us, we realize that the lives they lived, the things they achieved for God, and the suffering they endured were all done by faith, an unrelenting trust in and throwing oneself on God. Hebrews 11:1 defines such faith this way: "Now faith is the assurance of things hoped for, the conviction of things not seen."

Faith is not a feeling; it is a response we make and action we take, even when we can't figure everything out, because we believe that when God promises, He is telling the truth and can be both trusted and obeyed. Faith is a fundamental and resolute decision one makes to trust God without reservation. As Brennan Manning has said so well, "[Faith] is the spirit of those disciples of Christ who refuse to substitute the rhetoric of ideas for personal commitment."[34]

Take the time to read about the lives and choices of some of the people who make up this hall of faith found in Hebrews 11. Abraham had a lovely, secure home and material prosperity. But to respond positively to God's call on his life, he left it all and headed into an uncertain future. He could do that because he was banking on God's character, God's Word and God's promises, things he could not see. That is faith. Building on that faith, he found God faithful. In fact, at God's request, Abraham was willing to give up his son, Isaac, even though God's promises to him hinged on the descendents who would come through that son. Faith is the evidence of things not seen. Abraham believed that if he simply did what God said, God would work out the details, even if it took a miracle. That is faith. That is trusting God with abandon.

Look at Moses. Raised in the king's palace in Egypt, he lived like a prince. All the pleasures and opportunities that power and affluence bring were his. However, Hebrews 11:24-26 describes his choice of faith and explains the reason behind that choice.

"By faith, Moses, when he had grown up, refused to be called the son of Pharaoh's daughter, choosing rather to endure ill-treatment with the people of God, than to enjoy the passing pleasures of sin. He considered the reproach of Christ greater riches than the treasures of Egypt; for he was looking to the (future) reward."

While Moses refused the pleasures of sin for God's sake, Rahab, formerly a prostitute in Jericho, a city that came under siege by the nation of Israel, chose to leave a life of corruption and join the people of God. In doing so, she risked her life. However, although all appearances indicated that her life was in jeopardy from fellow residents of Jericho, the actions she took by deciding to believe what God had said actually spared her life, while the other residents of Jericho died at the hand of God's victorious people.

"And what more shall I say? For time will fail me if I tell of Gideon, Barak, Samson, Jephthah, of David and Samuel and the prophets, who by faith conquered kingdoms, performed acts of righteousness, obtained promises, shut the mouths of lions, quenched the power of fire, escaped the edge of the sword, from weakness were made strong, became mighty in war, put foreign armies to flight. Women received back their dead by resurrection; and others were tortured, not accepting their release, in order to obtain a better resurrection; and others experienced mockings and scourgings, yes, also chains and imprisonment. They were stoned, they were sawn in two, they were tempted, they were put to death with the sword. They went about in sheepskins, in goatskins, being destitute, afflicted, ill-treated (men of whom the world was not worthy), wandering in deserts and mountains and caves and holes in the ground. And all these, having gained approval through their faith, did not receive what was promised, because God had provided something better for us, so that apart from us they should not be made complete" (Hebrews 11:32-40).

There they are, says the writer, the well known and unknowns together, who lived and achieved for God and also endured suffering because they had one thing in common: they believed in God's love and trusted Him with abandon. They took God at His word. They relied on God's promises. Their lives show us the possibilities of our own faith. It is in that sense that this great cloud of witnesses shouts to us from the past as we are challenged to get into Jesus' life and follow Him, and the ensuing choices lead us through trials, difficulties, and even sacrifice. They are cheering from the stands in the stadium, "Go, go, go! You can do it! We did it. So can you! Trust in God! Follow Christ at all costs. Go, go, go!" Their cheering is thunderous.

That imagery reminds me of an unforgettable experience I had at a Promise Keepers Conference in the Minneapolis Metrodome. Toward the end of the event, the conference leaders invited all of the pastors in the crowd to come out of the stadium seats and onto the playing field of the arena because they wanted to honor us as pastors. As we made our way to the stadium floor, 60,000 men cheered and shouted, "We love you! Thank you! Keep going! Press on!" The cheering was enormous, the thunderous ovation deafening and moving. The energy and encouragement was revitalizing. As I stood there looking up, I imagined for a moment that these were those saints and martyrs who had gone before, who finished the course and kept the faith, now cheering us on. How powerfully that picture fired my faith and determination to follow Christ.

To the men and women who make up the "cloud of witnesses" from the past, it was a small thing for them to give up material goods, temporal ambitions and pleasures in order to respond to God's call and follow hard after Christ. By faith, they had set their sights on something much higher, something much better, based on the promises of God. And here is a most astonishing detail. Hebrews 11:39, 40 tell us that they have not received what they were shooting for yet—but they will one day, along with the rest of us who are faithful, on that day when Jesus returns and distributes rewards as we stand before Him. So they spur us on; they motivate us; they encourage us; they cheer for us. And they wait to receive their reward together with us when we see Christ face to face. Isn't that amazing?

The writer continues: Let those who have finished the race well, cheer you on to run and finish your race well. The best way to run and finish this marathon race of a lifetime of faith is to travel light and run with endurance (Hebrews 12:1b). Just as an athlete must divest himself of anything that would impede his progress, so must we. This especially applies to sin, since sin inevitably will cause us to trip up, stumble and fall. The text doesn't refer to particular besetting sins, but to sin itself as the trouble. Renounce all of it. Have nothing to do with any of it. It makes sense that sin has no place in the life of the person who is getting into Jesus' life. Therefore, no sin is insignificant or incidental. Is there anyone or any thing in your life that pulls your attention away from the Lord and fouls up your "running" as you follow Christ? Lay it aside no matter how appealing it is. Believe God's word when He promises, "It will be worth it!" Shun besetting sin. Turn away from distractions. Let go of doubts. Don't give up. Don't quit. Go for that "long obedience in the same direction" the way these "witnesses" did. "But that is so difficult," we are tempted to protest, until we recall the timely words of the hymn writer: *"Must I be carried to the skies on flowery beds of ease, while others fought to win the prize and sailed through bloody seas?"*

Heb.12: 2, 3 give us the secret to succeeding the way these fans of faith did.

"...fixing our eyes on Jesus, the author and perfecter of faith, who for the joy set before Him endured the cross, despising the shame, and has sat down at the right hand of the throne of God. For consider Him who has endured such hostility by sinners against Himself, so that you may not grow weary and lose heart."

This is most amazing. The things that were done by many of these witnesses, who now are cheering us on, were done *prior to* the coming of Christ. In that sense, it took more faith. They had less to go on than we do. They had to look forward to things promised which had not yet happened, things that they did not realize or receive in their entire lifetimes. We, on the other hand, can look to Jesus who has already blazed the trail for us perfectly. The writer and the fans of faith in the stadium surrounding us are saying to us: "Look at what Jesus did. He is the pioneer of perfect faith. He obeyed God the Father completely. He chose to endure the cross because that was necessary to the outcome, our salvation—pardon from sin and fellowship with God. But now Christ is exalted at the right hand of God the Father, and He calls us to enter into His life and into His race. Rivet your eyes on Jesus. He ran this race to a triumphant finish." While Jesus hung dying on the cross, taking your sins and mine on Himself, and it appeared that He had lost the race, His critics taunted, "He trusted in God (look at the good it did him)!" Now, in Christ's resurrection and exaltation, we exclaim, "He trusted in God (look at the good it did him—and us)!" In Revelation 3:21, Jesus says to us, *"He who overcomes, I will grant to him to sit down with Me on My throne, as I also overcame and sat down with My Father on His throne."* Wow.

After affirming that God maintains a "scroll of remembrance" for such faithful over-comers (Malachi 3:16), Brian Chapell notes this, "Confidence in heaven's memory grants earthly courage for divine purposes." Later he adds, "Because of its ever-lasting significance, no work done for God is trite, and no person who serves God will be forgotten."[35] No indeed. Rather, those faithful over-comers who ran their race faithfully and well will hear from the Savior, "Well done, good and faithful servant…Enter into the joy of your Master" (Matthew 25:21).

Notice that Hebrews 12:2 says, "Jesus…who for the joy set before Him endured the cross, despising the shame…" For Jesus this was all about joy. Sustained by indescribable heavenly joy, He weathered the with-ering brutality of Roman crucifixion, the oppressive weight of all our sins heaped on Him, and the relentless wrath of God directed against those sins. And Jesus tells us in John 15:11 that He wants His joy to be in us so that our joy would be full. He actually prays for this in John 17: 13 when He says to God His Father, "But now I come to you…that they may have My joy made full in themselves." You see, salvation is not only about getting our sins forgiven. As we have seen already, it is about entering into a relationship with Christ and having His likeness restored in us. God's gracious par-doning of our sin through Christ's sacrificial death on the cross gets the obstacles to the relationship out of the way so that our sharing in Christ's life and joy can begin. This does not mean that there is never sorrow or grief. After all, the Bible tells us that Jesus was "a man of sorrows, well-acquainted with grief" (Isaiah 53:3). But His joy superseded His sorrow because it was grounded in hope and anchored in unrelenting and undiminished trust in God's love and perpetual presence. When we have entered into Christ's life by faith, the reality of that relationship is the joy of the Lord, produced by His Spirit *within* us no matter what we are experiencing *without*. That is why the Apostle Paul could write to the Thessalonian Christians without contradicting himself, "You became imitators of the Lord, for you received the word in much afflic-tion with the joy of the Holy Spirit" (1 Thessalonians 1:6). This is not a picture of people inviting Jesus into their lives, to bless their plans and give them success. Rather, it is a picture of people who had set their sights on the Savior, got into His life and followed hard after Him because He had blazed the trail for them. Christ Himself is our inspiration. When our spirits flag, the witnesses who have gone before us point us to Christ and He fires us up. When trouble comes and we are distressed, like a child learning to swim in the arms of his father, we look into the face of Jesus and see that He is undisturbed. "I have you," He assures us. A sweet calm sweeps over our souls as we settle into the security of His embrace and whisper back to Him, "I trust in your love for me, Lord. I trust you completely."

"Look at Jesus," the writer of Hebrews implores us, "so that you don't lose heart and give up!" And we, cheered on by the fans of faith, and inspired by our trailblazing Savior, do exactly that, and go all out!

Think of it. At this very moment, that great cloud of witnesses is cheering us on to deny ourselves, get into Jesus' life, and follow Him, even if it involves sacrifice, pain, and loss. Living lives of self-denial, they, in the footsteps of their Savior, died deaths of self-sacrifice. Because they had entered into Jesus' life, they are promised an eternal reward.

Today there are all kinds of women and men and young people who, because they believe the promises of God, and trust in His love for them, have entered into Jesus' life, are living notable lives of faith and service, and have discovered the joy that comes only this way. There are Dennis and Barbara Sullivan, medical missionaries in Haiti, and Greg and Carolyn Kirschner, medical missionaries to Nigeria who have given up the promise of prosperous surgical practices in the United States of America to show indigent patients the reality and love of Christ in destitute and dangerous circumstances. There are Larry and Nancy Allen, who with their five children call impoverished Bangladesh their home in a culture that dares such missionaries to promote Christ, and that devalues the worth of women and deprives its citizens of every creature comfort. Yet, such obstacles quickly fade as yet another soul receives salvation by trusting in the loving sacrifice of Christ.

During a trip I took to Nairobi, Kenya, while meeting with a number of pastors and evangelists from all over the African continent, I was moved by this memorable prayer from a Congolese pastor who had suffered greatly in his service for Christ: "Lord, you be the needle and I will be the thread. With my life threaded into yours, you will lead the way and I will follow. I will go wherever you are going."

On January 2, 1956, five men, Pete Fleming, Ed McCully, Nate Saint, Roger Youderian, and Jim Elliot went to a little sand bar on the Curaray River in Ecuador and set up camp there in hopes of making contact with the Auca Indians in order to share with them the Gospel of Jesus Christ. They had spent much advance time and effort to pave the way for a meeting with these people. Then, on January 6, 1956, their hopes were realized when three of the Aucas stepped out of the jungle and spent several hours with the missionaries. While verbal communication was not possible, connections were made through gestures and signs. The Indians gave every impression that they trusted the missionaries even to the extent that one of them accepted a ride in Nate Saint's airplane. Yet, two days later, these five missionaries were speared to death.

If you were the wife, or sister, or daughter of these men, what would you do? Would you be angry with God, bitter toward the Auca people, and ready to throw in the towel on faith? Prepare to be startled. These are the very people—wives, sister, daughter of the martyred missionaries—who went to live with the Auca Indians in 1958, and in doing so, brought them the Gospel and led them to Jesus Christ. There was only one way that could happen. They looked not at themselves, but at Jesus Who had blazed the trail of faith for them. And roaring in their ears were the cheers of the fans of faith, among whom were their five loved ones who had died at the hands of the Aucas.

Still, most of us may not venture down such heroic paths. How do all these things apply to the life races we run day in and day out—lives that will never be recorded in the "Who's Who in the Hall of Faith"? The fact of the matter is that we have our own tests of faith that, while seeming to fall on a much lesser scale, nevertheless challenge *us* to "run with endurance" in a way that reflects well on the Savior we follow. You might be facing a life-threatening illness or debilitating health problems. You may be living with an alcoholic parent, going through a divorce or experiencing financial loss. Perhaps you are wringing your hands over a wayward son or daughter. Problems that challenge our faith and faithfulness are only a phone call or doctor's diagnosis away. Beyond all of these things are the challenges and losses we may face by faithfully obeying the commands of Christ and following Him without reservation.

As I write this, I am thinking of some of the tests of faith that have come my way from the earliest days of my following Jesus: a teacher badgering me with sarcasm in front of the rest of the class because I spoke favorably of God's actions and plans recorded in the Old Testament; a horrific auto accident that sent me crashing through a car windshield jeopardizing my life; co-workers in the corporation where I was employed alienating me because, as a Christian, I refused to "pad" my expense account; my son being sent into harm's way in Operation Iraqi Freedom; my tiny granddaughter being diagnosed with a rare and life-threatening disease for which there is no cure; a difficult diagnosis related to my own health; and, in light of these, something so seemingly petty as a neighbor directing his sump pump discharge directly into my yard! My response in each of these situations, great or small, speaks volumes to those who observe my life regarding my faith in Christ. A life lived faithfully in spite of suffering and loss is a very powerful witness to the reality of one's commitment to get into Jesus' life and follow Him. It is an indication of a race run well and also holds the certainty of finishing that race well.

There are the countless Christians who have not made missionary or other life-demanding ministries their vocations, or who do not live in environs where following Christ can jeopardize one's life. Yet, because they have gotten into Jesus' life and He into theirs, they bring the reality of Christ to the marketplaces, schools and neighborhoods of everyday America, day in and day out. Because they trust in God's love for them, they make tough and costly choices in order to follow Christ and carry out His calling on their lives. These have embraced Christ's mission of compassion and redemption. They realize that by getting into Jesus life, He has gotten into theirs. They believe Jesus' promise in John 14: 23, "If anyone loves me, he will keep My word; and My father will love him and We will come to him and make our home in him." They understand that God's residence in us makes our bodies His temple—a place of His perpetual presence and our ceaseless worship.

They have fixed their eyes on Jesus and are cheered on by the fans of faith. Are you among them?

So "let us run the race that we have to run with patient endurance, our eyes fixed and focused on Jesus, the pioneer and perfecter, the source and goal of our faith" as we are cheered on by our devoted forebears, the fans of faith . Run well. Finish well. And may those who come behind us find us faithful because we have gotten into Jesus' life, have trusted Him with abandon, and have followed hard after Him all our days.

PRAYER: *Dear Father, may we enter so fully into our Savior's life that He will be alive in us with joy indescribable, even in the midst of difficulty or adversity. As we trust in your love with both unrestrained enthusiasm and quiet confidence, may we be shaped into the likeness of our Lord Jesus in the very middle of who we are, that His joy might be in us and that our joy might be full to overflowing. May we join the great host of witnesses to Christ in such a way that those who come behind us will see the reality of His likeness and joy in us and affirm that we have indeed been faithful to Him. Amen.*

Endnotes

Chapter One

[1]Buchanan, Mark. *Your God is Too Safe.* Sisters, Oregon: Multnomah Publishers
[2]Richard Foster, Forward to Brennan Manning, *Ruthless Trust: The Ragamuffin's Path to God.* New York: HarperCollins. 2000. p. x.
[3]Colson, Charles and Fickett, Harold. *The Faith: What Christians Believe, Why they Believe it, and Why it Matters.* Grand Rapids, MI, Zondervan, 2008.

Chapter Two

[4]Francis Fukuyama, *Trust: The Social Virtues and the Creation of Prosperity.* New York: Simon and Schuster 2000. pp. 10ff.
[5]Scott McKnight, *The NIV Application Commentary: 1 Peter,* Grand Rapids, MI: Zondervan Publishing House. 1996. p. 176.

[6]Skip Hollandsworth, "Maybe a Miracle," *Reader's Digest,* Dec 2001, p. 119

[7]John White *The Fight,* Downers Grove, IL: Intervarsity Press. 1976. p. 115.

[8]Paul Tokunaga, Ed., with Jonathan Tran and Robbie Castleman, *Faith on the Edge: Daring to Follow Jesus.* Downers Grove, IL: Intervarsity Press, 1999. p. 185,

[9]Brennan Manning, *Ruthless Trust: The Ragamuffin's Path to God.* New York: HarperCollins 2000. p. 7

Chapter Three

[10]John Stott, *The Letters of John.* Grand Rapids, MI: Eerdmans Publishing House, 1988. p. 163.

[11]Martyn Lloyd-Jones, *The Cross.* Crossway Books, Westchester Illinois, 1986, p. 81.

Chapter Five

[12]John Stott. *Life in Christ,* Grand Rapids: MI: Baker Books, 1991 p.36.

[13]Thomas a' Kempis, *Imitation of Christ,* Nashville, TN: Thomas Nelson, 1999, pp. 48, 49.

[14]Martyn Lloyd-Jones, *The Cross,* Westchester, IL: Crossway Books 1986, pp. 187-188.

[15]Brennan Manning. *The Signature of Jesus.* Sisters, Oregon: Multnohmah Books, 1996. pp. 31-32.

Chapter Six

[16]Henri Nouwen. *The Road to Daybreak: A Spiritual Journey.* Doubleday, 1988.

Chapter Seven

[17]D.A. Carson, *The Expositors Bible Commentary, Vol. 8, Matthew.* Grand Rapids, MI: Zondervan Publishing House, 1984. p. 431.

[18]Charles Spurgeon. *Spurgeon's Sermons.* Grand Rapids, MI: Baker, 1989

[19]Oswald Chambers, *My Utmost for His Highest.* (c) 1935 by Dodd Mead & Co. renewed (c) 1963 by the Oswald Chambers Publications Assn., Ltd. Permission of Discovery House Publishers, Box 3566, Grand Rapids MI.

[20]Ibid.

[21]Charles Swindoll, *Improving Your Serve,* Waco, Texas: Word, Inc., p. 37.

Chapter Eight

[22]Ray Stedman, *Body Life,* Glendale, CA: Regal, 1972. pp.101-102

[23]Mark Buchanan, *Your God is Too Safe.* Sisters, Oregon: Multnomah Publishers, p.120.

[24]Helmut Thielicke, *Christ and the Meaning of Life,* Grand Rapids, MI: Baker Book House 1962, p.61.

Chapter Nine

[25]Cal Thomas interview, *Christianity Today,* April 25, 19994.

[26]Bill Hull. *The Complete Book of Discipleship.* Colorado Springs, NavPress 2006, pp. 38, 39.

Chapter Ten

[27]Richard Swenson, "Exhausted," *Newsweek,* March, 1995.

[28]Dallas Willard, *The Spirit of the Disciplines.* San Francisco: Harper & Row, 1988.

[29]Henri J.M. Nouwen. *Making All Things New: An Invitation to the Spiritual Life.* San Francisco: Harper &Row, 1981.

[30]Charles Spurgeon. "Spiritual Revival, the Want of the Church," *Spurgeon's Sermons.* Grand Rapids, MI: Baker, 1989.

[31]Leonard Ravenhill, *The Significance of Prayer* (as quoted in Dan Hayes, *Fireseeds of Spiritual Awakening,* Rev. ed., Dickinson Press, 1995, pp. 86, 87).

[32]Thomas Merton, *New Seeds of Contemplation,* New York: New Directions, 1961, p.35.

[33]Brother Lawrence, *The Practice of the Presence of God.* Translated by John J. Delaney, New York: Doubleday, 1977.

Chapter Twelve

[34]Brennan Manning, *Ruthless Trust: The Ragamuffin's Path to God.* New York: HarperCollins 2000. p.173.

[35]Brian Chapell. *Holiness by Grace,* Wheaton, IL: Crossway Books. 2001, p. 217.

[36]*Ibid.,* p. 224.

BIBLIOGRAPHY

BOOKS:

Brother Lawrence. *The Practice of the Presence of God*. Translated by John J. Delaney, NewYork: Doubleday, 1977.

Buchanan, Mark. *Your God is Too Safe*. Sisters, Oregon: Multnomah Publishers.

Carson D.A. *The Expositors Bible Commentary, Vol. 8, Matthew*. Grand Rapids, MI: ZondervanPublishing House,1984.

Chambers, Oswald. *My Utmost for His Highest*. (c) 1935 by Dodd Mead & Co., renewed (c) 1963 by the Oswald Chambers Publications Assn., Ltd. Permission of Discovery House Publishers, Box 3566, Grand Rapids MI 49501.

Chapell. Brian. *Holiness by Grace*, Wheaton, IL: Crossway Books. 2001.

Colson, Charles and Fickett, Harold. *The Faith*. Grand Rapids, MI: Zondervan Publishing House. 2008.

Dc Talk and The Voice of the Martyrs. *Jesus Freaks: Martyrs*. Bloomington, MN. Bethany House. 2005.

Foster Richard. Forward to Brennan Manning, *Ruthless Trust: The Ragamuffin's Path to God*. New York: HarperCollins, 2000.

Fukuyama, Francis. *Trust: The Social Virtues and the Creation of Prosperity*. New York: Simon and Schuster 2000.

Garland David. *The NIV Application Commentary, Mark*, Grand Rapids, MI: Zondervan Publishing House. 1996.

Hull, Bill. *The Complete Book of Discipleship*. Colorado Springs, CO: NavPress. 2006.

Lloyd-Jones, Martyn. *The Cross*. Westchester Illinois: Crossway Books 1986.

Manning, Brennan. *Ruthless Trust: The Ragamuffin's Path to God*. New York: HarperCollins 2000.

Manning, Brennan *The Signature of Jesus*. .Sisters, Oregon: Multnohmah Books, 1996.

McKnight, Scott. *The NIV Application Commentary: 1 Peter*, Grand Rapids, MI: Zondervan Publishing House. 1996.

Merton, Thomas. *New Seeds of Contemplation*, New York: New Directions, 1961.

Nouwen, Henri J.M. *Making All Things New: An Invitation to the Spiritual Life*. San Francisco: Harper &Row, 1981.

Spurgeon, Charles. *Spurgeon's Sermons*. Grand Rapids, MI: Baker, 1989

Stedman, Ray. *Body Life*, Glendale, CA: Regal, 1972.

Stott, John. *Life in Christ*, Grand Rapids, MI: Baker Books, 1991

Stott, John. *The Letters of John*. Grand Rapids, MI: Eerdmans Publishing House, 1988.

Swindoll, Charles, *Improving Your Serve*, Waco, Texas: Word, Inc., 1981.

Thielicke, Helmut. *Christ and the Meaning of Life*, Grand Rapids, MI: Baker Book House 1962.

Thomas a' Kempis. *Imitation of Christ*, Nashville, TN: Thomas Nelson, 1999.

Tokunaga Paul, Ed., with Jonathan Tran and Robbie Castleman, *Faith on the Edge: Daring to Follow Jesus*. Downers Grove, IL: Intervarsity Press, 1999.

White, John. *The Fight*, Downers Grove, IL: Intervarsity Press. 1976.

Willard, Dallas. *The Spirit of the Disciplines*. San Francisco: Harper & Row, 1988.

PERIODICLES:

Hollandsworth, Skip. "Maybe a Miracle," *Reader's Digest*, Dec 2001.

Swenson, Richard, "Exhausted," *Newsweek*, March, 1995.

LaVergne, TN USA
26 April 2010
180534LV00001B/2/P